Churchill Didn't Have a Tin Ear:

# Winston Churchill's Love of Music

Lena Walker —
with Best Wishes
Don Cusic
6/8/18

Don Cusic

ISBN: 978-0-9990537-1-3

Brackish Publishing
P.O. Box 120751
Nashville, TN 37212



Cover Design & Interior Layout: Priceless Digital Media

Production Coordinator: Jim Sharp, Sharp Management

# INTRODUCTION

Most of those who write about Winston Churchill write about his leadership during World War II. That is appropriate and as it should be because that is when Winston Churchill as a Great Man came into full bloom.

There are full length biographies examining his entire life and important passages in his life, such as his childhood, his experiences during World War I and Gallipoli and his "wilderness years." There are books on his paintings, his cigars and his life as a writer. Amongst those books, chapters and articles on his life, there is sometimes a mention of Churchill singing, or playing the gramophone, or his love of Music Hall songs.

In this book, I look at Churchill's love of music and the title of this book, *No Tin Ear: Winston Churchill and His Love of Music*, points out times when he listened to the gramophone or burst into song. This is not a topic that serious historians or biographers dwell on, although Churchill was well known for his love of music and singing. However, in this book I dwell on this aspect of Winston Churchill.

This is a small book about a large life but I hope it brings readers a little closer to Winston Churchill and perhaps allows readers a chance to enjoy the company of one of the most important, interesting, entertaining and fascinating figures in the twentieth century.

## Earliest Singing

Winston Churchill was born on November 30, 1874 in Blenheim Palace in Oxfordshire, England, the son of Lord Randolph Churchill, a prominent Tory politician, and Lady Jenny Churchill, an American.

At the end of 1877, the Churchills moved to Ireland, a month after Winston turned two. Randolph Churchill was often away from home and in a letter Jennie Churchill wrote to her husband she noted that "Winston has learned a new song, 'We will all go hunting today.'"

The song was about fox hunting and was written by W. Wilson.

## We'll All Go A-Hunting Today

(also known as "A Fine Hunting Day")

It's a fine hunting day, it's as balmy as May
The hounds to the village will come;
Every friend will be there, but all trouble and care
Will be left far behind them at home;
It's a-roaming along on the way,
Each one to the other did say,
We'll join the glad throng that goes laughing along,
And we'll all go a-hunting today!

CHORUS:
We'll all go a-hunting today,
All nature looks smiling and gay.
Let us join the glad throng that goes laughing along,
And we'll all go a-hunting today.

Farmer Hodge to his dame cries, "I'm sixty and lame,
Though hard times and rent I must pay;
I don't care a jot if I raise it or not,
For I must go a-hunting today.
There's a fox in the spinney-a-lying
We'll find him and get him away,
I'll make the first rush to ride hard for his brush,
For I will go a-hunting today."

CHORUS

The village bells chime, there's a wedding at nine,
The parson unites the fond pair;
He hears the sweet sound of the horn and the hounds,
And he knows it is time to be there;
He says, "For your welfare I'll pray,
Regret I no longer can stay;
You're safely made one and I must quickly be gone,
For I must go a-hunting today."

## St. George's School and Brighton

In 1882, Winston was sent to St. George's School in Ascot then, in 1884, was sent to school in Brighton. During his time at Blenheim, young Churchill heard the workers in the stables talking and singing and had "learned words and manners which were highly unsuitable for a young gentleman," stated Celia Sandys in her book *The Young Churchill*. Mr. Kynnersley, his school master at Brighton, "reacted with shock and apprehension against the not unlikely possibility that the entire school might adopt the spicy expressions and the readily imitable attitudes of stable lads. When Winston, who was quite tiny—he was only just eight years old—leapt around on a classroom table and recited to an attentive group of boys a little song from the stables. Mr. Kynnersley threated the use of the birch."

"At Brighton, young Churchill discovered concerts and pantomines," wrote Celia Sandys. Pantomines were musical comedy stage productions for family entertainment. They were often performed during the Christmas and New Year's season and included songs, skits, slapstick comedy, dancing and cross dressing. The audience was expected to participate in pantomines, singing along with songs and shouting out comments to the performers.

Young Winston wrote to his mother "there is a ripping good Pantomine down here" and noted "I am learning dancing now and like it very much indeed." He took piano lessons "but begged to be allowed to learn the cello or the violin instead," stated Sandys. His mother loved classical music but that "interested him very little." Instead, "Winston favored music hall tunes, for which he had a prodigious memory, or patter songs from the Savoy Operas of Gilbert and Sullivan that he loved to sing in his soft treble voice."

On February 12, 1885, Winston's mother and brother were in the audience when he appeared in a pantomime "as a woman 'Lady Bertha' & he acted quite wonderfully & looked so pretty." In 1887, Lady Randolph wrote to Lord Randolph that she took Winston to "a pantomime in Brighton where they hissed a sketch of you—he burst into tears-& then turned furiously on a man—who was hissing behind him--& said 'Stop that now you snob nosed Radical."

## British Music: A Brief History

During the mid-nineteenth and early twentieth century the Music Hall was a major source of popular entertainment in the United Kingdom. It was a type of variety show that featured musical acts as well as comedy and specialty acts, much like American vaudeville.

The Music Hall traces its roots back to early "pubs" or "public houses," which were bars or saloons that featured entertainment. The early Music Halls were not "theaters" because in a pub you could sit at a table, drink alcohol, eat and smoke while watching the entertainment. Theatres had more formal seating and the room for the bar was separate.

The Music Hall developed into larger establishments during the late nineteenth century, with room for 500 to 5000 people and evolved into a "theatre of varieties" with grand designs, spotlights, splendid and luxurious interiors and theatre seating.

During the early twentieth century popular Music Hall entertainers included Marie Dainton, Marie Lloyd, Arthur Roberts, Joe Elvin and Gus Elen. The demand for songs led to the application of copyright law for the compositions of songwriters and music publishers. During the days of the Music Hall, the sheet music business thrived and music publishers became profitable businessmen.

During World War I Music Hall songs like "Keep the Home Fires Burning," "Pack Up Your Troubles," "It's a Long Way to Tipperary," "We Don't Want to Lose You (But We Think You Ought To Go)," "What Did You Do in the Great War, Daddy," "I've Got a Bit of a Blighty One," "Jolly Good Luck to the Girl Who Loves a Soldier" and "Oh, It's a Lovely War" became popular. There were War Bond drives and recruitment drives during Music Hall performances during World War I.

The movies, then radio and the phonograph became popular during the first half of the twentieth century, which led to a decline in the Music Hall, although stars such as George Formby, Gracie Fields, Max Miller and Flanagan and Allen emerged.

The songs performed in Music Halls were written by songwriters, although early traditional folk songs were also heard. In the mid-nineteenth century, minstrel songs by Stephen Foster and others entered the Music Hall as well as Irish and European music. The "standard" Music Hall song featured a chorus, where the audience was invited to sing along, after verses by a solo performer. As ragtime and jazz developed, they became part of the Music Hall repertoire.

Comedy was broad and brash—often done by two people, a straight man and his wisecracking partner-- and specialty acts included magicians, cyclists, ventriloquists, sword swallowers, jugglers, plate spinners, strong men, fire eaters, trampoline and gymnast acts, animal acts and puppets. Those who attended a Music Hall performance were treated to a full variety show whose purpose was entertainment for the masses.

Music Hall shows were aimed primarily for working class Brits and a "general" audience; they were not staged for the upper class although many in the upper class held a guilty pleasure because they secretly enjoyed them. Many of the most popular songs were distinctly British, such as "Boiled Beef and Carrots," "Burlington Bertie from Bow," "Daddy Wouldn't Buy Me a Bow Wow," "I'm Henry the VIII, I Am," "Ta Ra Ra Boom-de-ay," and "Run, Rabbit, Run." Some of those songs, such as "I'm Henry the VIII" and "Leaning On the Lamp Post" later became pop hits during the British Invasion (sung by Herman's Hermits).

## H.M.S. Pinafore

Churchill wrote to his mother on January 12, 1888 and told her "I am going to a play called 'Pinafore' tonight. "Pinafore" was "H.M.S. Pinafore," a comic opera by Gilbert and Sullivan, the most popular composers of British comic operas during the late nineteenth century.

W.S. Gilbert (lyrics) and Arthur Sullivan (music) had written with others before stage producer Richard D'Oyly Carte brought them together in 1875 to write *Trial By Jury*. The opera was a success and Gilbert and Sullivan wrote 14 more comic operas before the end of the nineteenth century.

*H.M.S. Pinafore* satirizes the Royal Navy and the British obsession with class and social status. The plot involves the captain's daughter, who is in love with a lower class sailor, but her father wants her to marry the First Lord of the Admiralty. It premiered at the Opera Comique in London on May 25, 1878, and was Gilbert and Sullivan's first international hit. The show ran for 571 performances and, during the run, the show's promoter, Richard D'Oyly Carte, split from his investors, which led to Carte, Gilbert and Sullivan forming the D'Oyly Carte Opera company, which produced their following operas.

## HARROW

On April 17, 1888, Churchill entered Harrow and it was here he learned to memorize long sections of poetry and prose. It was also at Harrow that Churchill fell in love with the Harrow songs. The song "Five Hundred Faces," written by W. Howson and John Farmer, was traditionally sung on Speech Day by a new student.

# Five Hundred Faces

Five hundred faces, and all so strange!
Life in front of me, home behind
I felt like a waif before the wind
Tossed on an ocean of shock and change

Yet the time may come, as the years go by
When your heart will thrill
At the thought of the Hill
And the day that you came so strange and shy

A quarter to seven! There goes the bell!
The sleet is driving against the pane,
But woe to the sluggard who turns again
And sleeps not wisely but all too well!

Yet the time may come, as the years go by
When your heart will thrill
At the thought of the Hill
And the pitiless bell with its piercing cry

Nothing but proses and reps and con!
O for the future when I'm a man
With no more Virgil to learn and scan
And no one to say to me, "Please go on!"

Yet the time may come, as the years go by
When your heart will thrill
At the thought of the Hill
And the proses so long and the con so dry

"Raining in torrents again," they say,
The field is a slippery, miry marsh
But duty is duty, though sometimes harsh
And "footer" is "footer" whatever the day!

Yet the time may come, as the years go by
When your heart will thrill
At the thought of the Hill
And the slippery fields and the raining sky

Five hundred faces alive with glee!
Trials are over, the term is done
With all its glory and toil and fun
And boyhood's a dream of the past for me!

Yet the time may come, as the years go by
When your heart will thrill
At the thought of the Hill
And the wild regret of the last good-bye!

Churchill also loved "Forty Years On," written by E.E. Bowen and John Farmer, which was Harrow's "anthem."

## Forty Years On

Forty years on, when afar and asunder
Parted are those who are singing to-day
When you look back, and forgetfully wonder
What you were like in your work and your play,
Then, it may be, there will often come o'er you,
Glimpses of notes like the catch of a song
Visions of boyhood shall float them before you,
Echoes of dreamland shall bear them along,

Follow up! Follow up! Follow up!
Follow up! Follow up!
Till the field ring again and again
With the tramp of the twenty-two men
Follow up! Follow up!

Routs and discomfitures, rushes and rallies,
Bases attempted, and rescued, and won,
Strife without anger, and art without malice
How will it seem to you, forty years on?
Then, you will say, not a feverish minute
Strained the weak heart and the wavering knee
Never the battle raged hottest, but in it,
Neither the last nor the faintest, were we!

CHORUS:

O the great days, in the distance enchanted,
Days of fresh air, in the rain and the sun,
How we rejoiced as we struggled and panted
Hardly believable, forty years on!
How we discoursed of them, one with another,
Auguring triumph, or balancing fate
Loved the ally with the heart of a brother
Hated the foe with a playing of hate!

CHORUS

Forty years on, growing older and older,
Shorter in wind, as in memory long,
Feeble of foot, and rheumatic of shoulder,
What will it help you that once you were strong?
God give us bases to guard or beleaguer,
Games to play out, whether earnest or fun;
Fights for the fearless, and goals for the eager,
Twenty and thirty, and forty years on!

Another song Churchill loved to sing was "Here Sir!, written by E.W. Howson and Eaton Fanning.

## Here Sir!

Like an ancient river flowing
From the mountain to the sea
So we follow, coming, going
To the wider Life to be on our course
From the source
To the wider Life to be!
Here Sir! Here Sir! Here Sir! Here Sir!
On the top of Harrow Hill
Here Sir! Here Sir! Here Sir! Here Sir!
In the windy yard at Bill

Is it nought our long procession
Father, brother, friend and son
As we step in quick succession
Cap and pass and hurry on?
One and all at the call
Cap and pass and hurry on?
Here Sir! Here Sir! Here Sir! Here Sir!
On the top of Harrow Hill
Here Sir! Here Sir! Here Sir! Here Sir!
In the windy yard at Bill

One by one and as they name us
Forth we go from boyhood's rule
Sworn to be renown'd and famous

For the honour of the school
True as steel in our zeal
For the honour of the school
Here Sir! Here Sir! Here Sir! Here Sir!
On the top of Harrow Hill
Here Sir! Here Sir! Here Sir! Here Sir!
In the windy yard at Bill

So today and, oh! if ever
Duty's voice is ringing clear
Bidding men to brave endeavor
Be our answer, "We are here!"
Come what will, good or ill
We will answer "We are here!"
Here Sir! Here Sir! Here Sir! Here Sir!
On the top of Harrow Hill
Here Sir! Here Sir! Here Sir! Here Sir!
In the windy yard at Bill

## LECTURES

Churchill loved visiting lecturers and wrote in a letter, "To have an exciting story told by someone who is a great authority, especially if he has a magic lantern, is for me the best way of learning."

On Saturday, November 7, 1888 at Harrow, Churchill heard a lecture on the phonograph by Colonel Gouraud. "It was very amusing he astonished all sober-minded People by singing into the phonograph 'John Brown's Body lies—Mouldy in the grave and his soul goes marching on, Glory, glory, glory Hallelujah' and the Phonograph spoke it back in a voice that was clearly audible in the 'Speech Room.'" That event made a big impression on young Winston and the song remained one of his favourites.

## JOHN BROWN'S BODY

The song is about the abolitionist, John Brown, who led a raid on the army's arsenal at Harper's Ferry, Virginia in October, 1859. Brown thought his raid would lead to an armed slave revolt but his band of 22 was defeated by the U.S. Marines. Brown was captured and hung on December 2.

The tune to "John Brown's Body" came from American camp meetings during the late 1700s and early 1800s. Those camp meetings served as religious revivals in rural, early America. The earliest version of the tune was known as "Say, Brothers, Will You Meet Us." The "glory, glory Hallelujah" also came out of camp meetings during the early 1800s.

The song was good for marching and Union troops began singing it shortly after the American Civil War began. The tune to "John Brown's Body" was used for "The Battle Hymn of the Republic," with lyrics written by Julia Ward Howe in November, 1861 and published in the *Atlantic Monthly* in February, 1862.

# John Brown's Body

John Brown's body lies a-mouldering in the grave,
John Brown's body lies a-mouldering in the grave
John Brown's body lies a-mouldering in the grave
His soul's marching on

Glory, glory hallelujah
Glory, glory hallelujah
Glory, glory hallelujah
His soul is marching on

# Battle Hymn of the Republic

Mine eyes have seen the glory of the coming of the Lord
He is trampling out the vintage where the grapes of wrath are stored
He hath loosed the fateful lightning of His terrible swift sword
His truth is marching on

CHORUS:
Glory, Glory, hallelujah!
Glory, Glory, hallelujah!
Glory, Glory, hallelujah!
His truth is marching on

I have seen Him in the watch-fires of a hundred circling camps
They have builded Him an altar in the evening dews and damps
I can read His righteous sentence by the dim and flaring lamps
His day is marching on

REPEAT CHORUS:

I have read a fiery gospel writ in burnished rows of steel
"As ye deal with my contemners, so with you my grace shall deal
Let the Hero, born of woman, crush the serpent with his heel
Since God is marching on

REPEAT CHORUS:

He has sounded forth the trumpet that shall never call retreat
He is sifting out the hearts of men before His judgement seat
Oh, be swift, my soul, to answer Him! Be jubilant, my feet!
Our God is marching on

REPEAT CHORUS:

In the beauty of the lilies Christ was born across the sea
With a glory in His bosom that transfigures you and me
As He died to make men holy, let us die to make men free
While God is marching on
REPEAT CHORUS:

## The Phonograph

Thomas Edison invented the phonograph in 1877 at his home and workshop in West Orange, New Jersey. In August, 1878, the *Illustrated London News* carried a report of a phonograph demonstration made by Colonel Gouraud, Edison's London agent. The first known advertisement offering speaking machines for sale appeared in the U.K. in the very first edition of the *Boy's Own Paper* on January 18, 1879. The phonograph had become a sophisticated toy for the schoolboy or a means of making dolls talk, and even the novelty of those effects was quick to wear off. However, by October, 1878, all experiments with sound recording by Edison were laid aside to develop the electric light.

In October, 1887, Edison bounced back with his "Improved Phonograph" after the invention of a competing machine, the Graphophone by Chichester Bell and Charles Sumner Tainter, working at Alexander Graham Bell's laboratory. It was ready for the market by June 16, 1888. By this time the machines used solid wax cylinders. A scraper was provided for wiping off a recording to make room for another—so the 6 mm cylinder could be re-used many times.

Colonel Georges E. Gouraud was born in Niagara Falls, New York c. 1842. He became Edison's chief European representative at Beulah Hill, Upper Norwood, South London from 1878, where his house, "Little Menlo" (named after Edison's laboratory at Menlo Park, New Jersey), became a center for recording activities.

Colonel Gouraud, received a "Perfected Phonograph" on June 26, 1888; from that date his correspondence with Edison was conducted by cylinder, and he recorded the voices of Prime Minister William Gladstone, Sir Arthur Sullivan, Florence Nightingale, King Edward VII, Robert Browning and Alfred, Lord Tennyson.

On June 29, 1888, Colonel Gouraud set up a recorder in the press gallery of the Crystal Palace, London, to record parts of the Handel Festival's performance of "Israel in Egypt." This was the world's first "live" recording and the first recording of serious music.

A little over four months later, Colonel Gouraud was at Harrow School where he gave the demonstration of the phonograph that Churchill remembered so well.

## School Days

In a letter from Harrow, Churchill noted that "I rank as one of the most prominent trebles & am in what is called the nucleus of the choir...Of course I am so young that my voice has not yet broke and as trebles are rare I am one of the few."

"Winston was not to look back on his school days as the 'happiest days of his life,'" stated Cecelia Sandys. However, he "always enjoyed the Harrow songs."

"They have an incomparable book of school songs," remembered Churchill. "At intervals we used to gather in the Speech Room or even in our own Houses, and sing these splendid and famous choruses. I believe these songs are the greatest treasure that Harrow possesses."

One of his favorite school songs was "Left! Right!" written by E.W. Howson and Eaton Fanning.

# Left! Right"

Young Brown he was a little boy and barely four foot four,
But his manly bosom burned to join the Harrow Rifle Corps
So he went to see the Sergeant and he made a grand salute
And he said, says he, "I want to be a Volunteer Recruit."

CHORUS
Left! Right! Left! Right! Left! Left!
O the H.S.O.T.C.
'Tis a gallant sight to see,
As they swing along so gaily with the Band
With the trumpets blowing proud
And the big drum beating loud,
There is not another finer in the Land!
With the trumpets blowing proud
And the big drum beating loud
There is not another finer in the land

But the Sergeant shook his martial head, and shed a martial tear,
"You'll have to go away and grow and come another year."
So off he went with grim intent, and did his best and grew
And when the year was over he was nearly five foot two

REPEAT CHORUS
Then they stuck him in a uniform, and made him learn his drill
And double hard about the Yard and up and down the Hill
'Now by my troth," the Sergeant quoth, "If little Brown could grow
He'd make the smartest officer that ever you did know."

REPEAT CHORUS

And grow he did and on the Range so well he practiced up
A "bull" he got, with every shot, and won the Spencer Cup
And when he tried for Sandhurst, he was sure as fate to pass,
For wasn't he a member of the Harrow Army Class?

REPEAT CHORUS

And now he's in a Regiment a-fighting for the Crown
And soon he'll be a K.C.B. and Major-General Brown
So listen all, both great and small, and may there be some more
To rally round to the bugle sound and join the Rifle Corps!

REPEAT CHORUS:

"Giants" was another of his favorite school songs:

## GIANTS

There were wonderful giants of old, you know,
There were wonderful giants of old;
They grew more mightily, all of a row,
Than ever was heard or told;
All of them stood their six feet four,
And they threw to a hundred yards or more,
And never were lame or stiff or sore;
And we, compar'd to the days of yore,
Are cast in a pigmy mould.
For all of we, whoever we be,
Come short of the giants of old, you see.

There were splendid cricketers then, you know,
There were splendid cricketers then;
The littlest drove for a mile or so,
And the tallest drove for ten;
With Lang to bowl and Hankey to play,
Wenn and Walker to score and stray,
And two that I know, but may not say
But we are a pitiful race of clay,
And never will score again
For all of we, whoever we be
Come short of the giants of old, you see

There were scholars of marvelous force, you know,
There were scholars of marvelous force;
They never put *un* when they should put *ou*
And the circle they squared, of course.
With Blayds and Merivale, Hope, Monro,
Ridley and Hawkins, years ago,
And one that I rather think I know—
But we are heavy and dull and slow,
And growing duller and worse;
For all of we, whoever we be,
Come short of the giants of old, you see

But I think all this is a lie, you know,
I think all this is a lie;
For the hero-race may come and go
But doesn't exactly die!
For the match we lose and win it again,
And the Balliol comes to us now and then,
And if we are dwarfing in bat and pen,
Down to the last of the Harrow men,
We will know the reason why!
For all of we, whoever we be
Come up to the giants of old, you see.

## SANDHURST

On January 1, 1893, Winston Churchill entered the Royal Military Academy in Sandhurst and graduated the next year.

On January 24, 1895, Churchill's father, Lord Randolph Churchill, died. That same year Churchill went to Cuba to observe the Spanish fight Cuban guerrillas and filed reports about the conflict for the *Daily Graphic* newspaper. It was there that he began a life-long love affair with Cuban cigars.

In 1896, Churchill was assigned to Bombay in British India where he fought against Pashtun tribes and filed reports for English newspapers. His reports are compiled and published as Churchill's first book, *The Story of the Malakand Field Force.*

In 1898, Churchill transferred to Egypt and took part in the British re-conquest of Sudan. He participated in one of the last British cavalry charges in history at the Battle of Omdurman.

## ENTERS POLITICS

On May 5, 1899, Churchill resigned from the British Army in order to begin his political career but lost his first campaign for Parliament as a Conservative. However, Churchill impressed many with his campaigning skills.

After he lost the election, Churchill went by ship to South Africa to report on the Second Boer War. He was captured but escaped and received a commission in the South African Light Horse.

The following year he returned to England and won a seat for Oldham in Parliament with the Conservative Party.

There were complaints about entertainment and liquor by some citizens "of which Mrs. Ormiston Chant is a fair specimen," wrote Churchill. Churchill disliked "impetuous reformers" and read in the *Daily Telegraph* that a meeting for the "Entertainments Protection League," an "organization founded with the express purpose...to resist and counter the intolerance of Mrs. Chant and her backers" would be held. Churchill volunteered his services and "In due course I received an answer on impressively headed notepaper...inviting my attendance at the first meeting of the Executive Committee."

Churchill spent three days preparing a speech should he be called to deliver one, carefully avoiding every word beginning with "s" because of his lisp. He took a hansom cab from Waterloo to Leicester Square where he was "surprised and a little disconcerted at the dingy and even squalid appearance of these back streets." In Leicester Square he met "face to face the Founder of the new body. He was alone, I was upset; but concealing my depression under the fast-vanishing rays of hope, I asked, 'When do we go up to the meeting?'"

The gentleman replied, "there's only you and me" so "I bade him a restrained but decisive farewell, and walked out into the street with a magnificent oration seething within my bosom and only half a crown in my pocket."

Leaving the scene, Churchill "encountered a side of life that he had hitherto avoided" and stated "I did what I had never done before or since. I had now reached the Strand. I saw the three golden balls hanging over Mr. Attenborough's well-known shop." In the pawn shop he pawned some possession for money and "received one of those tickets which hitherto I had only heard of in music-hall songs.... and sallied forth."

He wrote to his mother that "Mrs. Ormiston Chant and her 'prowling prudes' succeeded in persuading the authorities to separate the promenade from the offending bars with canvas screens. These were demolished by an angry crowd and ...the bars were once more united with the promenade to which they had ministered so long..In these somewhat unvirginal surroundings I now made my maiden speech."

## A Liberal

In 1906, Churchill switched from the Conservative to the Liberal Party.

## Marriage

On September 12, 1908, Churchill married Clementine Hozier in St. Margaret's Church at Westminster Abbey. He had known her for four years.

## In the Cabinet

In 1910, Churchill was promoted to Home Secretary, responsible for the internal affairs in Britain.

## Swansea

On August 14, 1908, Winston Churchill spoke at the Albert Hall in Swansea about the German threat to peace. Before he began his talk on Germany, he said "I can assure you I am very glad indeed to come here today. I am glad to come to Swansea. I am glad to come to the miners' demonstrations. (Cheers.) This is the third time in the course of the summer months that I have had the honour to address a Welsh audience. I have come to the conclusion that I must be considered to be making myself a favourite down here. (Laughter and cheers.) I shall always be glad to come back to hear you sing (cheers)—to hear you sing those beautiful hymns and songs with so much harmony and so much unison, because one feels in listening to your singing the strength and the virtue of the Welsh race." (Cheers.)

## First Lord of the Admiralty

On September 1, 1911, Winston Churchill was made First Lord of the Admiralty, in charge of the Royal Navy. In April, the following year, Churchill "bought a Welte Steinway piano on the installment plan, only to return it one month later and ask to be let out of his commitment." Churchill wanted to be able to play and 15 years later, in 1927, "he again bought on installment from Harrods a new Welte piano—this time a pianola, a self-playing 'player piano'—only to once again abandon the plan and return it."

On January 13, 1915, he presented his plan for an assault on the Dardanelles and Gallipoli, which was launched on April 25. The attempted assault lasted until January 9, 1916 and ended in disaster. Thousands of British soldiers were dead in Turkey, which was then part of the Ottoman Empire. The assault was a disaster and Churchill was blamed; it was the lowest point of his career. He was demoted and decided to join the war effort, serving on the Western Front.

After he arrived on the front, he decided to boost morale of the troops and organized a day of sports and a concert. One of his soldiers, John McGuire, remembered that "A piano had been procured from somewhere, new songs were practiced and various games were devised with somewhat macabre local touches, such as 'the bomb throwers."

McGuire stated that "Winston Churchill was the world's most horrible singer, and he started to sing 'Me Old Tarpaulin Jacket' and it was terrible, and the boys they were clapping and they were as pleased as could be. He was a real man's man.'"

## TARPUALIN JACKET

A "tarpaulin jacket" was made of heavy fabric and treated with tar so it was rainproof.

The words of that song were written by G.J. Whyte-Melville and the tune was composed by Charles Coote, who was half owner and director of the Coote and Tinney Band, a premier dance orchestra in London during the 1850s. George John Whyte-Melville was a British novelist who graduated from Eton in 1839. He was a captain in the Coldstream Guards in 1846 and retired from the army in 1849.

## THE TARPAULIN JACKET

A tall stalwart lancer lay dying,
And as on his deathbed he lay,
To his friends who around him were sighing,
These last dying words he did say;
Wrap me up in my tarpaulin jacket
And say a poor buffer lies low;
And six stalwart lancers shall carry me
Carry me with steps solemn, mournful and slow.

Had I the wings of a little dove,
Far far away would I fly; I'd fly
Straight for the arms of my true love
And there I would lay me and die.

Wrap me up in my tarpaulin jacket
And I say a poor buffer lies low;
And six stalwart lancers shall carry me
Carry me with steps solemn, mournful and slow

Then get you two little white tombstones
Put them one at my head and my toe, my toe,
And get you a penknife and scratch there,
Here lies a poor buffer below.
Wrap me up in my tarpaulin jacket
And say a poor buffer lies low;
And six stalwart lancers shall carry me
Carry me with steps solemn, mournful and slow

And get you six brandies and sodas,
And set them all out in a row, a row,
And get you six jolly good fellows
To drink to this buffer below.
Wrap me up in my tarpaulin jacket
And say a poor buffer lies low;
And six stalwart lancers shall carry me
Carry me with steps solemn, mournful and slow

And then in the calm of the twilight
When the soft winds are whispering low, so low,
And the darkening shadows are falling,
Sometimes think of this buffer below.
Wrap me up in my tarpaulin jacket
And say a poor buffer lies low;
And six stalwart lancers shall carry me
Carry me with steps solemn, mournful and slow

## Singing Songs

In his book, *In Search of Churchill*, author Martin Gilbert noted that "All his life, Churchill enjoyed singing the music hall songs of his youth, and his old school songs: their actual words, which most people could only hum, he knew by heart."

In his large biography of Churchill, Gilbert noted that "In his old age Churchill wanted to make a gramophone record of all the songs of his youth and army days, having remembered them with a perfect recall for the words and verses (if not perfect pitch). To the best of my knowledge the record was never made."

Here are some of the songs that Winston Churchill knew and loved.

## Whiter Than Whitewash on the Wall

Whiter than the whitewash on the wall,
Whiter than the whitewash on the wall,
Oh wash me in the water
That you washed your dirty daughter in,
And I shall be whiter than the whitewash on the wall.
Oh, on the wall, on the wall,
Oh, wash me in the water
That you washed your dirty daughter in,
And I shall be whiter than the whitewash on the wall.
(Sometimes the line "your dirty daughter" was sung "the colonel's daughter.")

## Songs During World War I

There were a number of songs that were popular during the World War I period that Churchill knew and loved; in fact, many of his favorite songs came from that period. The most popular song of World War I was "It's a Long Way to Tipperary," written by Jack Judge and Henry James "Harry" Williams. "Tipperary" is a county in Ireland and was sung by the Irish regiment of the Connaught Rangers and quickly picked up by other units in the British army. Songwriter Jack Judge's parents were Irish and his grandparents came from Tipperary. Judge and his co-writer, Harry Williams, wrote 32 music hall songs.

The song was first performed on a British music hall stage in 1912 by Jack Judge in Stalybridge at the Grand Theatre.

## It's a Long Way to Tipperary

Up in mighty London came an Irish man one day
As the streets are paved with gold, sure, everyone was gay
Singing songs of Piccadilly, Strand and Leicester Square
Till Paddy got excited, then he shouted to them there:

CHORUS:
It's a long way to Tipperary
It's a long way to go
It's a long way to little Mary

To the sweetest girl I know
Goodbye, Piccadilly
Farewell, Leicester Square
It's a long, long way to Tipperary
But my heart's right there

Paddy wrote a letter to his Irish Molly-O
Saying, "Should you not receive it, write and let me know!"
"If I make mistakes in spelling, Molly, dear," said he
"Remember, it's the pen that's bad, don't lay the blame on me!"

CHORUS:

Molly wrote a neat reply to Irish Paddy-O
Saying "Mike Maloney wants to marry me, and so
Leave the Strand and Piccadilly or you'll be to blame
For love has fairly drove me silly, hoping you're the same

CHORUS:

## Keep the Home Fires Burning

Another Churchill favorite song was "Keep the Home Fires ('Till the Boys Come Home)," later simply known as "Keep the Home Fires Burning." It was written by Ivor Novello (music) and an American friend of Novello's, Lena Guilbert Ford (lyrics) and published on October 8, 1914 by a London firm. The song was recorded by James F. Harrison (1915), Stanley Kirkby (1916) and John McCormack (1917).

# Keep the Home Fires Burning

They were summoned from the hillside
They were called in from the glen
And the country found them ready
At the stirring call for men
Let no tears add to their hardships
As the soldiers pass along
And although your heart is breaking
Make it sing this cheery song

Keep the home fires burning
While your hearts are yearning
Though your lads are far away
They dream of home
There's a silver lining
Through the dark clouds shining
Turn the dark cloud inside out
Till the boys come home

Overseas there came a pleading
"Help a nation in distress"
And we gave our glorious laddies
Honour made us do no less
For no gallant son of freedom
To a tyrant's yoke should bend
And a noble heart must answer
To the sacred call of "Friend"

Keep the home fires burning
While your hearts are yearning
Though your lads are far away
They dream of home
There's a silver lining
Through the dark clouds shining
Turn the dark cloud inside out
Till the boys come home

## If You Were the Only Girl (in the World)

The song "If You Were the Only Girl (In the World)" debuted in the musical revue *The Bing Boys Are Here*, which premiered in London at the Alhambra Theatre on Leicester Square on April 19, 1916. It was written by Nat D. Ayer (music) and Clifford Grey (lyrics).

Sometimes when I feel bad and things look blue
I wish a girl I had, say one like you
Someone within my heart to build her throne
Someone who'd never part, to call my own

If you were the only girl in the world
And I were the only boy
Nothing else would matter in the world today
We could go on loving in the same old way
A garden of Eden just made for two
With nothing to mar our joy

I would say such wonderful things to you
There would be such wonderful things to do
If you were the only girl in the world
And I was the only boy
No one I'll ever care for dear, but you
No one I'll fancy, therefore love me do
Your eyes have set me dreaming all night long
Your eyes have set me scheming, right or wrong
If you were the only girl in the world
And I were the only boy
Nothing else would matter in the world today
We could go on loving in the same old way

## Irving Berlin

Irving Berlin's "Alexander's Ragtime Band" and "Everybody's Doin' It" were popular songs in British Music Halls. "When the Midnight Choo-Choo Leaves For Alabam" was also popular in those Music Halls but it came after a tragedy in Berlin's life.

Irving Berlin fell in love with Dorothy Goetz and married her in February, 1912; however, on their honeymoon in Cuba a typhoid epidemic broke out and Dorothy fell ill. They went back to New York where her condition worsened and she died in July, about five months after their wedding. Berlin was distraught and found himself unable to write hit songs; his songs written during that period seemed a bit lifeless.

Finally, Berlin sat down and wrote "When I Lost You," a song about his wife and the only song that Berlin wrote that he admitted came from his personal life. That song rejuvenated his writing and he then wrote "When the Midnight Choo-Choo Leaves for Alabam," which was an up tempo hit for him in the United States as well as in English Music Halls.

## When the Midnight Choo-Choo Leaves for Alabam

I've had a mighty busy day
I've had to pack my things away
Now I'm going to give the landlord back his key
The very key that opened up my dreary flat
Where many weary nights I sat
Thinking of the folks down home who think of me
You can bet you'll find me singing happily
CHORUS:
When the midnight choo-choo leaves for Alabam
I'll be right there, I've got my fare
When I see that rusty-haired conductor man
I'll grab him by the collar and I'll holler
"Alabam!" "Alabam!"
That's where you stop your train that brings me back again
Down home where I'll remain where my honey-lamb am
I will be right there with bells when that old conductor yells
"All aboard!" "All aboard!"
"All aboard for Alabam"
The minute that I reach the place

I'm goin' to overfeed my face
Cause I haven't had a good meal since the day I went away
I'm gonna kiss my Pa and Ma
A dozen times for ev'ry star
Shining over Alabama's new mown hay
I'll be glad enough to throw myself away

"A Life on the Ocean Wave" was a poem written by Epes Sargent that was set to music by Henry Russell. It was first published in 1838.

## A Life on the Ocean Wave

A life on the ocean wave
A home on the rolling deep
Where the scattered waters rave
And the winds their revels keep
A life on the ocean wave
A home on the rolling deep
Where the scattered waters rave
And the winds their revels keep

Like an eagle caged I pine
On this dull unchanging shore
Oh, give me the flashing brine
The spray and the tempest roar
A life on the ocean wave
A home on the rolling deep
Where the scattered waters rave

And the winds their revels keep
The winds, the winds,
The winds their revels keep
The winds, the winds,
The winds their revels keep

The land is no longer in view
The clouds have begun to frown
But with a stout vessel and crew
We'll say let the storm come down
The land is no longer in view
The clouds have begun to frown
But with a stout vessel and crew
We'll say let the storm come down

And the song of our hearts shall be
While the winds and waters rave
A life on the heaving sea
A home on the bounding wave
And the winds their revels keep
The winds their revels keep
The winds, the winds,
The winds their revels keep

The song "Lily of Laguna" was written by an American, Eugene Augustus Ruhlmann, who adopted the stage name Eugene Stratton. Stratton, born in 1861, moved to England in 1880 where he became the song and dance man in the Moore and Burgess Minstrel Show. "Coon songs," which stereotyped blacks in a racist manner, were quite popular during the end of the nineteenth and early twentieth centuries. "Lily of Laguna" is a "coon song" and Stratton, who wrote it in 1898, performed in blackface. As the twentieth century progressed, early "coon songs," such as "Bill Bailey Won't You Please Come Home" and others, lost their image as a "coon song" and were accepted as popular songs.

The "Laguna" of this song is a village of North American cave dwellers, although the exact location is vague.

## Lily of Laguna

She's my lady love, she is my dove
My baby love
She's no girl for sittin' down to dream
She's the only Queen Laguna knows.
I know she likes me
I know she likes me because she said so
She is my Lily of Laguna.

She is my Lily and my Rose
She's my lady love
She is my dove
My baby love

She's no girl for sittin' down to dream
She's the only Queen Laguna knows
I know she likes me
I know she likes me because she said so
She is my Lily of Laguna
She is my Lily and my Rose
She's my lady love
She is my dove
My baby love
She's no girl for sittin' down to dream
She's the only Queen Laguna knows

I know she likes me
I know she likes me because she said so
She is my Lily of Laguna.
She is my Lily of Laguna.
She is my Lily of Laguna.

## CHARTWELL

In 1924 Churchill moved into Chartwell, which would be his home for the remainder of his life. In a letter on April 17 to his wife, Clementine (who disliked Winston purchasing Chartwell). Churchill wrote about his new living arrangements, "I drink champagne at all meals & buckets of claret & soda in between...In the evening we play the gramophone and Mah Jonngg (sic)."

The following year he began writing *The World Crisis*, his history of World War I. During that summer, his wife,

Clementine, was hit by a bus in London and left for Venice to recover. Meanwhile, Churchill continued dictating *The World Crisis* and Martin Gilbert noted that "each night he would turn out the lights and listen to music on the wireless with his brother Jack."

## RE-JOINS THE CONSERVATIVES

In 1925, Churchill re-joined the Conservative Party after he became an independent.

The low point of his political career came during the 1930s when he was estranged from the Conservative leadership. He turned his attention to writing and wrote M*arlborough: His Life and Times*" about one of his ancestors.

In 1931 he spoke against the independence movement in India, which was led by Mohandas Gandhi, and the next year warned about Germany, which was re-arming. He spoke for boosting Britain's air defense and in support of King Edward VIII during the abdication crisis. Churchill's support of King Edward, who abdicated the throne to marry Wallis Simpson, an American divorcee, hurt his career.

## LONDON IN WAR

Britain declared war on Germany on September 3, 1939 and during those early years of the war, London was full of entertainment. In his book, *London at War*, Philip Ziegler stated that "it was a need to dance that above all consumed every level of London society in those first months. The large public dance halls were full as never before." American broadcaster Edward Murrow reported that "Customers want to dance. Places are jammed nearly every night. People come early and stay late. Uniforms and civilian clothes are about evenly divided, but practically no one wears formal evening dress."

In London, "There were more dance bands playing in the West End than before the war; even the most sedate restaurant found it necessary to have a small orchestra," stated Ziegler.

The first hit song of the war, "We're going to hang out our washing on the Siegfried Line" was sung by Inge Anders at the Café de Pris. Theatres closed and then re-opened and the musicals *Me and My Girl* and *Under Your Hat* were popular. Enlistments and the draft meant that the BBC Symphony lost 30 of its 120 musicians. The Royal Albert Hall was closed but re-opened in March, 1940.

## Early in the War

On April 3, 1940, the Ministerial Defense Committee was formed with Churchill, now First Lord of the Admiralty, as its chair. He then replaced Lord Chaatfield as Minister for Coordination of Defense.

On May 1, Germany invaded Belgium, France, Luxembourg and the Netherlands.

On May 10, 1940, Winston Churchill replaced Neville Chamberlain as Prime Minister.

## Prime Minister

On the day that Winston Churchill became Prime Minister—May 10, 1940--the Germans began a massive invasion of Luxembourg, Belgium, the Netherlands and France. The Dutch defeated the Germans at the Battle for The Hague; on May 12 the Belgians blew up all the bridges over the Meuse River in an attempt to halt the German army as the Battle of Hannut began. On May 13 a German Panzer corps broke through at Sedan, France and Churchill gave his "blood, toil, tears, and sweat" speech in the House of Commons. That same day the Dutch lost the Battle of the Grebbegerg. The next day the Luftwaffe carpet bombed Rotterdam and the Netherlands surrendered to Germany.

Churchill appealed to President Franklin Roosevelt and Canada for aid. The Rotterdam Blitz resulted in the surrender of the Dutch army and the German army crossed the Meuse River. On May 16 Churchill visited Paris and received a report on the French war. That same day the Belgian government left Belgium for Bordeaux, France; on May 17 the Germans entered Brussels and took Antwep while a new French government was formed by Paul Reyneau; in the government was 84-year-old Marshal Petain, the French hero of World War I. On May 19, German troops attacked Amiens, Rommel's forces surrounded Arras and German forces reached Noyelles on the Channel.

## The War

On May 20, German troops took Abbeville; three days later, Oswald Mosely, leader of the fascists in Britain was jailed along with his wife. On May 25, the British and French forces retreated to Dunkirk and Hitler, sensing he had them trapped, called a halt to the German army's advance and ordered the Luftwaffe to attack. There were sporadic bombings by the German Luftwaffe in England while in the north, the Soviet Union prepared for a takeover of the Baltic States. On May 26, Calais surrendered to the Germans but there was a bright spot when "Operation Dynamo" began the evacuation of 340,000 troops from Dunkirk; the Dunkirk evacuation continued until June 3 under heavy bombing by the Luftwaffe.

On May 28, Belgium surrendered. In an intense discussion by the British Cabinet to seek an armistice with the Germans, led by Lord Halifax and Neville Chamberlain, Churchill prevailed with a vote to continue fighting. By June 3, 224,686 British troops, along with 121,445 French and Belgium troops had been successfully evacuated while the Germans bombed Paris. On June 10, Italy declared war on France and the United Kingdom, Norway surrendered and on June 11, the Siege of Malta began and the French government moved to Tours. On June 12, over 10,000 British troops were captured at Saint-Valeryen-Caux and on June 13, German troops occupied France and the French government moved to Bordeaux. On May 14 there was a total blockage of the Baltic States by the Soviet fleet with Soviet troops on the Baltic borders. On June 15, the Soviets gave Lithuania an eight hour deadline to surrender, then entered the country. In France, British troops began an evacuation from the ports in western France in a movement known as "Operation Ariel."

## CHURCHILL AT CHEQUERS

On Saturday, June 15, Churchill was at Chequers and John Colville wrote in his diary that "After tea Winston dictated long telegrams to Roosevelt and to the Dominions....pointing out that he had now got to face the most trying ordeal of heavy bombing and saying to all that he personally was convinced that the carnage and destruction in this country would bring the U.S. into the war. He said that the French condition for carrying on had been a promise of active U.S. support...."If words counted, we should win this war," he said as a comment on his own telegraphic efforts."

The group at Chequers—Churchill, Duncan and Diana Sandys, Professor Lindemann and Coleville—had dinner at 9:30 p.m. "It was at once the most dramatic and the most fantastic evening I have ever spent," wrote Colville. There were telephone calls and telegrams before dinner: "from Bordeaux: the position was deteriorating fast and the request to be allowed to make a separate peace was being put in a more brutal form. I imparted this to Winston who was immediately very depressed. Dinner began lugubriously, W. eating fast and greedily, his face almost in his plate, and every now and then firing some technical question at Lindemann, who was quietly consuming his vegetarian diet. The Sandys and I sat silent because our spasmodic efforts at conversation were not well received. However, champagne and brandy and cigars did their work and we soon became talkative, even garrulous. Winston, in order to cheer himself and us up, read aloud the messages he had received from the Dominions and the replies he had sent to them and to Roosevelt. 'The war is bound to become a bloody one for us now,' he said, 'but I hope our people will stand up to bombing and the Huns aren't liking what we are giving them. But what a tragedy that our victory in the last war should have been snatched from us by a lot of softies.'"

After dinner, Churchill and Duncan Sandys walked in the rose garden. "It was light and deliciously warm, but the sentries, with tin helmets and fixed bayonets, who were placed all round the house, kept us fully alive to the horrors of reality," wrote Colville, who was making and receiving phone calls and then going out to find Churchill in the rose garden.

Talking about the French attitude, which was resigning itself to defeat, Churchill told Colville, "Tell them that if they let us have their fleet we shall never forget, but that if they surrender without consulting us we shall never forgive. We shall blacken their name for a thousand years!" but then countered, "Don't, of course, do that just yet."

"He was in high spirits, repeating poetry," recorded Colville, "dilating on the drama of the present situation, maintaining that he and Hitler only had one thing in common—a horror of whistling—offering everybody cigars, and spasmodically murmuring, "Bang, Bang, Bang, goes the farmer's gun, run rabbit, run rabbit, run, run, run."

## Run, Rabbit, Run

"Run, Rabbit, Run" was a popular song sung by the Music Hall act Flanagan and Allen. It was written by Noel Gay, who wrote the music, and Ralph Butler, who wrote the lyrics. It was originally written for *The Little Dog Laughed*, a show by Noel Gay, which opened on October 11, 1939.

The song became popular during World War II and Flanagan and Allen often changed the lyrics to "Run Adolf, Run Adolf!"

On the farm, every Friday
On the farm, it's rabbit pie day.

So, every Friday that ever comes along,
I get up early and sing this little song

Run rabbit, run rabbit, Run! Run! Run!
Run rabbit, run rabbit, Run! Run! Run!
Bang! Bang! Bang! Bang!
Goes the farmer's gun.
Run, rabbit, run, rabbit, run

Run rabbit, run rabbit, Run! Run! Run!
Don't give the farmer his Fun! Fun! Fun!
He'll get by
Without his rabbit pie
So run rabbit, run rabbit, Run! Run! Run!

Some interesting side notes: In Paul McCartney's song, "Band On The Run" by Wings he has the lyrics "For the rabbits on the run." "Run, Rabbit, Run" was popular with school children during World War II, which is when Paul McCartney, born in 1941, no doubt first heard it. Pink Floyd's album *Dark Side of the Moon* has a song, "Speak to Me/Breathe" which has the lyrics, "Run, Rabbit, Run" in it and The Clash, in their song, "Bankrobber," sing "Run, Rabbit, Run."

## Churchill Speaks to Parliament

Hitler was planning an invasion of Britain, beginning on September 15. During the early days of August, the Soviet Union annexed Lithuania, Latvia and Estonia, claiming that the Soviet border extended to the Baltic Sea. On August 13, the German Luftwaffe began a two-week assault on British airfields, known as "The Battle of Britain." Germany was using its air force to prepare for their invasion of Britain but the British used "radar," a new technology they had developed to thwart the German's efforts. On August 18 there was heavy fighting in the Battle of Britain with the Germans suffering severe losses.

On August 20, 1940, John Colville went to the House of Commons to hear Churchill's speech, which included the lines "never in the field of human conflict has so much been owed by so many to so few" about the Royal Air Force pilots in the Battle of Britain.

The speech "was less oratory than usual and the point of chief interest to the House was the account of the bargain with America about the lease of air-bases in the West Indies (he did not divulge what we hoped to get as a quid pro quo)," wrote Colville. "On the whole, except for bright patches—like that about 'the Fuhrer's reputation for veracity,' which had a great success—the speech seemed to drag and the House, which is not used to sitting in August, was languid. The P.M. ended by comparing Anglo-American co-operation (will it one day be unity?) to the Missouri river and said, "Let it roll on!"

Colville drove Churchill back in the car and "he sang 'Ole Man River' (out of tune) the whole way back to Downing Street."

## Old Man River

The song was written by Jerome Kern (lyrics) and Oscar Hammerstein II (music) for the musical *Show Boat*, which debuted in New York on December 27, 1927. The most famous version is by Paul Robeson from the 1936 film. In the first staging of the musical the song was sung by Jules Bledsoe. Robeson sang the song in the London production in 1928 and again in the Broadway revival of the show in 1932. The song was originally written in dialect but later versions "cleaned up" the lyrics.

Ol' man river, dat ol' man river
He must know sumpin' but don't say nuthin'
He jes keeps rollin'
He keeps on rollin' along

## London Bombed

On September 7, 1940, the German Luftwaffe began bombing London and continued bombing with only one night off for 57 days. In October, there was nocturnal bombing almost every night with German planes attacking not only London but also Liverpool, Bristol, Cardiff, Portsmouth, Plymouth, Birmingham, Coventry, Belfast, Glasgow, Manchester and other ports. By the time they finished, over a million houses had been destroyed and over 40,000 civilians were killed.

## The End of 1940

In November, 1940, Churchill, despite concerns from the military, sent troops from North Africa to Greece.

President Franklin Roosevelt requested the resignation of American Ambassador to Great Britain, Joseph P. Kennedy on December 1 after Kennedy, in a newspaper interview, stated "Democracy is finished in England."

On December 5, the German cities of Dusseldorf and Turin were bombed by the Royal Air Force and the next day troops from India, in addition to British troops, began an offensive against the Italian army in Egypt. On December 16, British planes dropped bombs on Mannheim, Germany during a night raid.

## Visits Harrow

On December 18, Winston Churchill, with his old school friend Leo Amery, came to Harrow for a visit. The visit came after the Secretary of State for India, who was a Governor of the Harrow School, told Churchill the school would love for the Prime Minister to visit. Churchill replied that he would only go if he could listen to the school songs. He requested they sing "When Raleigh Rose."

## When Raleigh Rose

When Raleigh rose to fight the foes,
We sprang to work and will
When glory gave to Drake the wave
She gave to us the Hill
The ages drift in rolling tide
But high shall float the morn
A-down the stream of England's pride,
When Drake and we were born

CHORUS:
For we began when he began
Our times are one
His glory thus shall circle us
Till time be done

The Avon bears to endless years
A magic voice along,
Where Shakespeare strayed in Stratford's shade
And waked the world to song
We heard the music soft and wild
We thrilled to pulses new
The wings that reared the Avon's child
Were Herga's nurses too

CHORUS
Guard, guard it well, where Sidney fell
The poet-soldier's grave
Thy life shall roll, O royal soul
In other hearts as brave
While thought to wisdom wins the gay
While strength upholds the free
Are we the songs of yesterday
Or heirs of thine and thee?

In the Speech Room, there were songs sung, including "Stet Fortuna Domus," with another verse added at the end in Churchill's honor.

## Stet Fortuna Domus

Pray, charge your glasses gentlemen
And drink to Harrow's honour
May Fortune still attend the Hill
And Glory rest upon her!
The world outside is wondrous wide
But here the world is narrow
One magic thrall unites us all
The name and fame of Harrow

Now fancy leans to other scenes
Where first we learnt to stammer
The elements of Greek and "Tique"
The mysteries of Grammar.
And bearded men are boys again
In fourth-form coat and collar
And on our lips are mellow quips
Of dominie and scholar

Forgotten cheers are in our ears
Again we play our matches
And memory swells with wizard spells
Our bygone scores and catches
Again we rush across the slush
A pack of breathless faces

And charge and fall and see the ball
Fly whizzing through the bases
Tonight we praise the former days
In patriotic chorus
And celebrate the Good and Great
Who trod the Hill before us
Where Sheridan and Peel began
In days of Whig and Tory
Where Ashley vow'd to serve the crowd
And Byron woke to glory

So once again your glasses drain
And may we long continue
From Harrow School to rise and rule
By heart and brain and sinew
And as the roll of Honour's Scroll
Page after page is written
May Harrow give the names that live
In Great and Greater Britain.

In Churchill's honor, another verse was added to the song.

Not less we praise in darker days
The leader of our nation,
And Churchill's name shall win acclaim
From each new generation
While in this fight to guard the Right
Our country you defend, Sir
Here grim and gay we mean to stay
And stick it to the end, Sir.

The visit to Harrow seemed to give him strength, especially after singing the school songs. His son Randolph, who accompanied him on the visit, later wrote "The stirring patriotism these verses evoked, abided with him forever and was the mainspring of his political conduct." The Prime Minister told Randolph, "Listening to those boys singing all those well-remembered songs I could see myself fifty years before singing those tales of great deeds and of great men and wondering with intensity how I could ever do something glorious for my country."

Not long after his visit to Harrow, Churchill's assistant, John Colville, took a telegram sent by President Roosevelt upstairs for Churchill, who was sitting in his bath singing "St. Joles" "at the top of his voice."

Churchill read the telegram, gave Colville instructions concerning the message and continued singing "St. Joles" as he told Colville "what an inspiration the Harrow songs had been to him throughout his life."

# St. Joles

When time was young and the school was new
(King James had painted it bright and blue)
In sport or study, in grief or joy
St. Joles was the friend of the lazy boy
He helped when the lesson at noon was said,
He helped when the Bishop was fast in bed
For the Bishop of course was master then
And Bishops get up at the stroke of ten

CHORUS:
St. Joles hooray, and St. Joles hooroo
Mark my word if it don't come true
In sport or study, in grief or joy
St. Joles is the friend of the lazy boy.

If an "a" was possibly short or long
St. Joles would whisper it right (or wrong)
If ever an "e" provoked a doubt
St. Joles's Lexicon helped it out
Perhaps it wasn't in page or print
But it hinted a probable friendly hint
And often indeed, if I must confess
It was like to a sort of a kind of guess.

CHORUS

But there came a morning of fear and dread
When the Bishop was up, and the Saint in bed
And all the boys, from bottom to top
Instead of bishop, pronounced bishop!

However the guilty class might try
They lengthened "o" and they shortened "i"
And the Bishop with righteous anger flames
And off he went and he told King James

CHORUS

O then, King James, in his wrath and ire
Degraded St. Joles to Joles Esquire
And now to punish the awful crime
They get up at seven in winter time
And oft the vowels in prose and song
St. Joles's Lexicon tells you wrong
And if you believe me, down at play
There's always fog on St. Joles's day

CHORUS

In the days after Churchill's visit to Harrow, the Luftwaffe conducted bombing raids on Manchester December 22-24.

## CHRISTMAS 1940

Churchill was at Chequers on Christmas Eve to spend the holiday with his family. John Colville was there and wrote in his diary that, after dinner, "the shorthand writer was dismissed and we had a sort of sing-song until after midnight. The PM sang lustily, if not always in tune." Vic Oliver, the husband of Churchill's daughter, Sarah, was billed as "England's Favourite American Comedian." He played Viennese waltzes while Churchill "danced a remarkably frisky measure of his own in the middle of the room."

On Christmas morning, Churchill did work and dictation and then the family had a large turkey for lunch. After lunch, there were no official visitors and the group listened to the King's speech over the BBC. It was family time and Churchill's three daughters, Diana, Sarah and Mary as well as sons-in-law Duncan Sandys and Vic Oliver and daughter in law, Pamela (his son Randolph was in Cairo) enjoyed an evening of Oliver playing the piano and singing which led to another sort of sing-song until after midnight."

Four days later, on December 29, a German air raid over London resulted in St. Paul's Cathedral being hit and damaged. On New Year's Eve, the Germans bombed London, hitting The Old Bailey, the Guildhall and eight churches built by Christopher Wren, which were destroyed or badly damaged. Bombs were dropped by the Royal Air Force on factories in Bremen, Germany.

## Harry Hopkins Visits

On Monday, January 8, 1941, Harry Hopkins, President Roosevelt's trusted friend and emissary, arrived in Britain where, two days later, he spent three hours with Churchill at Downing Street. During the weekend, Churchill and Hopkins went to Ditchley where they discussed Britain's needs.

President Roosevelt had decided to provide assistance to Britain with a "lend-lease" agreement whereby America would lease or "rent" military hardware manufactured in the United States to Britain with no payments made until the end of the war. Roosevelt had to be careful helping Britain because the "America First" movement, led by aviator Charles Lindberg, insisted that the United States should stay on its own shores and not become involved in foreign wars. In order to obtain the military hardware that the United States manufactured, Britain had to pay debts she owed to the United States in gold as well as through the sale of commercial assets owned by Britain in the United States.

In Roosevelt's year end radio address he had announced that "We must be the arsenal of democracy." On January 10, the day Churchill and Hopkins met, the bill for "lend-lease" was introduced in Congress.

On January 12, Hopkins went to Bletchley and learned of the Enigma Code, which scrambled German communications. The United States had broken the code for Japanese communication and that was sent to Britain as Washington and London agreed to pool their intelligence resources.

During the time Churchill and Hopkins were together, German planes took control of the air over the Mediterranean, threatening Malta and a German bomb exploded outside the Bank of England, killing 57 and injuring 69. The next day, January 12, British and Australian troops prepared for an assault on Tobruk, held by the Italians and on January 13 there were heavy night raids by German planes on Plymouth. There were also heavy night raids on Malta while in East Africa, the British attacked Eritrea. Hitler and Italian dictator Mussolini met in Germany and Hitler agreed to provide aid to the Italians in North Africa.

Harry Hopkins spent twelve evenings with Churchill and at Chequers, during the last weekend, he presented Churchill with a large box of gramophone records, "all American tunes or ones with an Anglo-American significance," observed Eric Seal, Churchill's principal Private Secretary. Seal wrote home that "We had these until well after midnight, the PM walking about, sometimes dancing a pas-seul, in time with the music. We all got a bit sentimental & Anglo-American, under the influence of the good dinner & the music."

On Saturday, January 25—Hopkins last weekend with Churchill—the Prime Minister gave a talk on the BBC.

The idea that Germany might invade Ireland as a diversion was brought up by General Dill. During the rest of the evening, spent in the Great Hall at Chequers, "the gramophone played and the P.M. in the intervals of discoursing to Hopkins or Dill, tripped a little measure."

## Early 1941

At the beginning of March, 1941, British commandos carried out an attack on the oil facilities in Norway and some British troops left Libya to help in Greece; on March 7 the first troops landed in Greece. The next day, German bombing in London hit Buckingham Palace.

On Sunday, March 9, French General Charles de Gaulle, who had met with Churchill, left and Churchill then met with Colonel Donovan and discussed Donovan's tours in the Balkans and Paninsular. Sir Alan Brooke came for dinner and spent the night while Professor Lindenham and Alastair Forbes, who were also there for dinner, held a "flippant conversation about metaphysics, solipsists and higher mathematics." After dinner, "the gramophone played marches and old-fashioned songs of a martial kind (such as the P.M. loves)" while Churchill gave "a display of arms drill with his big game rifle." The group retired for bed at the early hour of 11:30 p.m.

The next day, March 10, Portsmouth was hit by heavy bombing from the Germans; on March 11 President Roosevelt signed the Lend Lease Act, which had been passed by Congress allowing Britain, China and other allies to purchase military equipment with payments delayed until after the war.

On March 30, 1941, Jock Colville wrote in his diary "This has been a wonderful week-end, the culmination of a week of victories." Visiting with Churchill were the American Ambassador John Winant, Averill Harriman, the Menzies and the Cranbornes.

Churchill thought that progress in the war would have an effect on Japan and had written to Matsoke, the Japanese Foreign Minister, who was the "moving spirit behind Japan's decision to join the Berlin-Rome Axis." Japan wanted to become friends with the Soviet Union to "isolate the U.S.A." so Matsoke went to Berlin where Hitler "told him nothing of his plan to invade Russia." That made Matsoke look "foolish when, on reaching Moscow, he signed a treaty with the Soviet Union just before it was attacked by his Axis allies." That forced Matsoke to resign his position.

Churchill asked, "Will Germany, without the command of the sea or the command of the British daylight air, be able to invade and conquer Great Britain in the spring, summer or autumn of 1941? Will Germany try to do so? Would it not be in the interests of Japan to wait until these questions have answered themselves? He asks seven other equally pertinent questions and concludes: "From the answers to these questions may spring the avoidance by Japan of a serious catastrophe, and a marked improvement in the relations between Japan and the two great sea powers of the West."

Churchill told Colville he "was now sure Germany would attack Yugoslavia before Greece or Turkey" and was "very hopeful on that front." Churchill sent several telegrams to Roosevelt and others and had "spent much of the week-end pacing—or rather tripping—up and down the Great Hall to the sound of the gramophone (playing martial airs, waltzes and the most vulgar kind of brass-band songs) deep in the thought all the while."

## Spring, 1941

On Easter Sunday, April 13, 1941, John Colville recorded that, after Churchill took a nap, Australian Prime Minister Menzies "arrived for dinner, at which only the P.M., Mary, Harriman and Tommy were present in addition. Afterwards we talked, pulled Mary's leg and played the gramophone. The P.M. worked till 2.15 a.m.

General Rommel attacked Tobruk on April 14, 1941 but was forced to retreat; the next day British destroyers intercepted an Afrika Korps convoy and sank all German transports and three Italian vessels. On April 17 Yugoslavia surrendered to

Germany; the next day Greek Prime Minister Alexandros Koryuzis committed suicide and the British planned an evacuation of Greece. There was heavy damage from German air raids in London on April 19.

On April 25, Rommel defeated the British at Halfaya Pass, near the Egyptian border and the next day moved into Egypt but the British continued to hold Tobruk and the Germans ceased attacks.

The Greek government was evacuated to Crete, which Churchill was determined to defend.

On April 29, Churchill appealed to Stalin again "to desist from the unilateral imposition of Soviet will in Poland, and also in Yugoslavia." That evening, after dinner at Chequers, "Churchill was watching a film of *The Mikado* and singing each of the songs when there was a telephone call from General Alexander. The film was stopped. The German armies in Italy had surrendered unconditionally. The war in Italy was over.

## NOEL COWARD

In July, 1941: Noel Coward's *Blithe Spirit* opened in London.

*Blithe Spirit* was Noel Coward's most enduring work. It premiered on the London stage in 1941 and Coward toured with the play during 1942. His cabaret act, honed during wartime tours, became a supreme success.

Noel Coward was a flamboyant dandy, a young man from the London suburbs who was taken up by the upper classes. Churchill loved his songs.

Coward's first experience acting came when he was seven; his first professional engagement came in January, 1911, when he was twenty. He was drafted in 1918 but declared unfit for active service because of health reasons.

Coward wrote short stories for magazines before he began writing plays; his first two plays, *Ida Collaborates* (1917) and *Women and Whiskey* (1918) were written with Esme Wynee. His first solo effort, written in 1918, was *The Rat Trap* and in 1920 he starred in a play he wrote, *I'll Leave It To You*. His first financial and critical success was *The Vortex*, written in 1924. That created a demand for more plays and songs from Coward.

In June, 1925, Coward had four shows running in theatres on the West End: *The Vortex*, *Fallen Angels*, *Hay Fever* and *On With the Dance*. In 1928, his hit song, "A Room With a View" was written for his musical, *This Year of Grace*. His song "I'll See You Again" came from *Bitter Sweet* and "Mad Dogs and Englishmen" came from *Words and Music*.

During the abdication crisis of 1936, when Edward decided to marry the divorcee Wallis Simpson, a constitutional crisis was created over who could be king. Coward differed sharply with Churchill, who supported Edward VIII's wish to marry "his cutie." Coward felt the king was irresponsible and told Churchill "England doesn't wish for a Queen Cutie."

King George VI wanted to award a knighthood to Coward in 1942 but was dissuaded by Churchill. The official reason was that Coward had been fined 200 pounds sterling for "contravening currency regulations" but, in fact, Churchill thought that Coward's flamboyant lifestyle would create a backlash.

Churchill felt that Coward could best serve his country by entertaining troops and the home front rather than in the intelligence world. "Go and sing to them when the guns are firing—that's your job!" Churchill told Coward, who followed his advice, for the most part. However, During World War II, Coward secretly worked for British intelligence, using his celebrity to influence public opinion in America through his stage act.

Famous songs that Coward wrote include "London Pride," "Don't Let's Be Beastly to the Germans," "Mad Dogs and Englishmen," "The Party's Over Now," "Dearest Love (Operetta)," "Dear Little Café," "Men About Town," "Twentieth Century Blues," "Uncle Harry," "There Are Bad Times Just Around the Corner," "Dance, Little Lady," "Has Anybody Seen Our Ship?" "I Went to a Marvelous Party," "Nina," "A Bar on the Piccola Marina" "Why Must the Show Go On?" and "Sail Away."

## Chequers, July, 1941

On Wednesday, July 9, 1941, Churchill and most of his family went to Chequers. Jock Colville was with them and recorded in his diary that, after dinner, Churchill talked about the political futures of Anthony Eden and Oliver Lyttelton. Churchill stated that Eden was "not supported in the House or in the party although personally he, Winston, admired his great moral and physical courage. 'He would equally well charge a batter or go to the stake for his principles—even though the principles might be wrongly conceived and he might charge the battery from the wrong angle,'" observed Churchill. Colville noted that Churchill and Archie Sinclair talked "till 2 a.m. while I played the gramophone for them." Colville recorded that Churchill "thought that when the war was over there should be an end to all bloodshed, though he would like to see Mussolini, the bogus mimic of Ancient Rome, strangled like Vercingetoriz in old Roman fashion. Hitler and the Nazis he would segregate on some island, though he would not so desecrate St. Helena." Colville added that "The P.M. inveighed against defeatism and said it would be better to make this island a sea of blood than to surrender if invasion came" and that he had received a copy of a letter sent by French politician Paul Reynaud to French General Phillipe Petain where Reynaud said that "after the Franco-Germany Armistice England would have 'her neck wrong like a chicken in three weeks.'"

## Atlantic Charter

On Saturday, August 16, 1941, after President Roosevelt and Churchill met in Newfoundland and drew up the "Atlantic Charter," John Colville recorded in his journal "The reactions to the Churchill-Roosevelt meeting are now crystallising and the significance of the declaration is more appreciated as the initial disappointment that something more startling did not emerge wears off. At the Ministry of Information Brendan provided a display of the films of the Prime Minister's voyage which have just been flown back to London. They were not yet cut or edited and some of the effects produced—in particular the singing of "Onward Christian Soldiers" at the service on H.M.S. Prince of Wales—were almost unbearably funny."

Churchill chose three songs for the service on the quarterdeck, "For Those in Peril on the Sea" (also known as "Eternal Father, Strong to Save"), "Onward Christian Soldiers" and "O God, Our Help in Ages Past."

# For Those in Peril on the Sea

This song was written by William Whiting, in 1860, inspired by Psalm 107. In was popularized by the navys in Britain and the United States.

Eternal Father, Strong to Save
Whose arm hath bound the restless wave
Who bidd'st the mighty ocean deep
Its own appointed limits keep
Oh, hear us when we cry to Thee
For those in peril on the sea

O Christ! Whose voice the waters heard
And hushed their raging at Thy word
Who walkedst on the foaming deep
And calm amidst its rage didst sleep

Most Holy Spirit! Who didst brood
Upon the chaos dark and rude
And bid its angry tumult cease
And give, for wild confusion, peace
Oh, hear us when we cry to Thee
For those in peril on the sea

O Trinity of love and power
Our brethren's shield in danger's hour
From rock and tempest, fire and foe,
Protect them wheresoe'er they go
Oh, hear us when we cry to Thee
For those in peril on the sea

# Onward, Christian Soliders

The words to “Onward, Christian Soldiers” were written in 1865 by Sabine Baring-Gould with the music composed in 1871 by Arthur Sullivan in the country home of Ernest Clay Ker Seymer.

The lyrics were originally written to the melody of Haydn’s “Symphony in D, No. 15” but did not catch on until Sullivan wrote the tune, which he originally called “St Gertrude” before it was set to the words of ‘Onward Christian Soldiers.’

Onward, Christian soldiers
Marching as to war
With the cross of Jesus
Going on before
Christ, the royal Master
Leads against the foe
Forward into battle
See His banners go

CHORUS: Onward, Christian soldiers
Marching as to war
With the cross of Jesus
Going on before

At the sign of triumph
Satan’s host doth flee
On then, Christian soldiers
On to victory
Hell’s foundations quiver
At the shout of praise

Brothers, lift your voices
Loud your anthems raise

REPEAT CHORUS

Like a mighty army
Moves the Church of God
Brothers, we are treading
Where the saints have trod
We are not divided
All one body we
One in hope, in doctrine
One in charity

REPEAT CHORUS

What the saints established
That I hold for true
What the saints believed
That I believe too
Long as earth endureth
Men the faith will hold
Kingdoms, nations, empires
In destruction rolled

REPEAT CHORUS

Crowns and thrones may perish
Kingdoms rise and wane
But the Church of Jesus
Constant will remain
Gates of hell can never
'Gainst that church prevail
We have Christ's own promise
And that cannot fail

REPEAT CHORUS

Onward then ye people
Join our happy throng
Blend with ours your voices
In the triumph song
Glory, laud and honor
Unto Christ the King
This through countless ages
Men and angels sing

## Oh, God, Our Help in Ages Past

This is an Isaac Watts hymn, inspired by Psalm 90. The first line "Our God" was changed to "O God" by John Wesley in his 1738 hymnal *Psalms and Hymns*.

Isaac Watts paraphrased biblical psalms, breaking from the tradition of singing them word for word as they were written. He published this hymn originally in his *The Psalms of David Imitated in the Language of the New Testament* in 1719.

The melody "St. Anne" is generally used for these lyrics; that tune was composed by William Croft in 1708

Oh God, our help in ages past
Our hope for years to come
Our shelter from the stormy blast
And our eternal home

Under the shadow of Thy throne
Still may we dwell secure
Sufficient is Thine arm alone
And our defence is sure

Before the hills in order stood
Our earth received her frame
From everlasting Thou art God
To endless years the same

Thy Word commands our flesh to dust
Return, ye sons of men
All nations rose from earth at first
And turn to earth again

A thousand ages in Thy sight
Are like an evening gone
Short as the watch that ends the night
Before the rising sun

The busy tribes of flesh and blood
With all their lives and cares
Are carried downwards by the flood
And lost in following years

Time, like an ever rolling stream
Bears all its sons away
Then fly, forgotten, as a dream
Dies at the opening day

Like flowery fields the nations stand
Pleased with the morning light
The flowers beneath the mower's hand
Lie withering ere 'tis night

Our God, our help in ages past
Our hope for years to come
Be Thou our guard while troubles last
And our eternal home

## SEPTEMBER, 1941

A German U-boat fired on the USS Greer on September 4, 1941, the first time an American warship was attacked by a German U-boat, which led to American ships providing convoy duties between the United States and Europe. The next day Germany occupied Estonia and on September 7, Royal Air Force bombers hit Berlin. On September 8 the siege of Leningrad began and the day after that President Roosevelt ordered the United States Navy to shoot on sight if any ship or convoy was threated, which led to the U.S. Naval Command ordering an all out war on Axis shipping in American waters on September 26,

On Sunday, September 27, Churchill entertained guests and, after discussing politics and various British politicians, reminisced to Jock Colville "about Harrow, where he said he had spent the unhappiest days of his life, and told how he and F.E. Smith had been booed when they went there in 1912. However he was going down again to hear the songs (he repeated several word-perfect by heart) and would recall me from wherever I then might be so that I could accompany him."

## A SECOND VISIT TO HARROW

Winston Churchill returned to Harrow on October 29, 1941 to hear the old school songs again. He spoke to the boys, stating,

"Almost a year has passed since I came down here at your Head Master's kind invitation in order to cheer myself and cheer the hearts of a few of my friends by singing some of our own songs. The ten months that have passed have seen very terrible catastrophic events in the world—ups and downs, misfortunes—but can anyone sitting here this afternoon, this October afternoon, not feel deeply thankful for what has happened in the time that has passed and for the very great improvement in the position of our country and of our home? Why, when I was here last time we were quite alone, desperately alone, and we had been so for five or six months. We were poorly armed. We are not so poorly armed today; but then we were very poorly armed. We had the unmeasured menace of the enemy and their air attack still beating upon us, and you yourself had had the experience of this attack; and I expect you are beginning to feel impatient that there has been this long lull with nothing particular turning up!"

He continued, "We must learn to be equally good at what is short and sharp and what is long and tough. It is generally said that the British are often better at the last. They do not expect to move from crisis to crisis; they do not always expect that each day will bring up some noble chance of war; but when they very slowly make up their minds that the thing has to be done and the job put through and finished, then, even if it takes months—if it takes years-they do it."

"Another lesson I think we may take, just throwing our minds back to our meeting here ten months ago and now, is that appearances are often very deceptive and, as Kipling well says, we must '...meet with Triumph and Disaster

And treat those two imposters just the same.'

"You cannot tell from appearances how things will go. Sometimes imagination makes things out far worse than they are; yet without imagination not much can be done," then he stated "Surely from this period of ten months this is the lesson: never give in, never give in, never, never, never, never—in nothing, great or small, large or petty—never give in except to convictions of honour and good sense. Never yield to force; never yield to the apparently overwhelming might of the enemy. We stood all alone a year ago, and to many countries it seemed that our account was closed, we were finished....Very different is the mood today. Britain, other nations thought, had drawn a sponge across her slate. But instead our country stood in the gap. There was no flinching and no thought of giving in; and by what seemed almost a miracle to those outside these Islands, though we ourselves never doubted it, we now find ourselves in a position where I say that we can be sure that we have only to persevere to conquer."

Churchill then turned his attention to the extra verse that was added to "Stet Fortuna Domus" during his last visit, stating "You sang here a verse of a School Song; you sang that extra verse written in my honour, which I was very greatly complimented by and which you have repeated today."

The verse was:

Not less we praise in darker days
The leader of our nation,
And Churchill's name shall win acclaim
From each new generation
While in this fight to guard the Right
Our country you defend, Sir
Here grim and gay we mean to stay
And stick it to the end, Sir.

"There is one word in it I want to alter," said Churchill, "I wanted to do so last year, but I did not venture to. It's the line 'Not less we praise in darker days.' I have obtained the Head Master's permission to alter 'darker' to 'sterner': 'Not less we praise in sterner days.'

"Do not let us speak of darker days; let us speak rather of sterner days. These are not dark days: these are great days—the greatest days our country has ever lived; and we must all thank God that we have been allowed, each of us according to our stations, to play a part in making these days memorable in the history of our race."

## HOUSE OF COMMONS OF CANADA

In Ottawa, Churchill spoke to the House of Commons of Canada on December 30, 1941. He thanked the Canadians for their help in the war effort and then said, "We did not make this war, we did not seek it. We did all we could to avoid it. We did too much to avoid it. We went so far at times in trying to avoid it as to be almost destroyed by it when it broke upon us. But that dangerous corner has been turned, and with every month and every year that passes we shall confront the evil-doers with weapons as plentiful, as sharp, and as destructive as those with which they have sought to establish their hateful domination."

Churchill told the assembly that he had spent the week with President Roosevelt, "that great man whom destiny has marked for this climax of human fortune. We have been concerting the united pacts and resolves of more than thirty States and nations to fight on in unity together and in fidelity one to another, without any thought except the total and final extirpation of the Hitler tyranny, the Japanese frenzy, and the Mussolini flop."

"There shall be no halting, or half measures, there shall be no compromise, or parley," continued Churchill. "These gangs of bandits have sought to darken the light of the world; have sought to stand between the common people of all the lands and their march forward and only when the earth has been cleansed and purged of their crimes and their villainy shall we turn from the task which they have forced upon us, a task which we discharge. According to my sense of proportion, this is no time to speak of the hopes of the future, or the broader world which lies beyond our struggles and our victory. We have to win that world for our children. We have to win it by our sacrifices. We have not won it yet. The crisis is upon us. The power of the enemy is immense. If we were in any way to underrate the strength, the resources or the ruthless savagery of that enemy, we should jeopardize, not only our lives, for they will be offered freely, but the cause of human freedom and progress to which we have vowed ourselves and all we have. We cannot for a moment afford to relax. On the contrary we must drive ourselves forward with unrelenting zeal. In this strange, terrible world war there is a place for everyone, man and woman, old and young, hale and halt; service in a thousand forms is open. There is no room now for the dilettante, the weakling, for the shirker, or the sluggard.... The enemies ranged against us, coalesced and combined against us, have asked for total war. Let us make sure they get it."

Churchill then brought an old Music Hall performer into his talk, stating "That grand old minstrel, Harry Lauder—Sir Harry Lauder, I should say, and no honour was better deserved—had a song in the last War which began, 'If we all look back on the history of the past, we can just tell where we are.'"

Churchill then looked back in his speech and talked of the invasion of Poland, the defeat or Norway, Denmark, Holland and Belgium and the French surrender. Churchill said of the surrender of France to Germany that "When I warned them that Britain would fight on alone whatever they did, their generals told their Prime Minister and his divided Cabinet, 'In three weeks England will have her neck wrung like a chicken.' Some chicken! Some neck!"

## Christmas and New Year's: 1942-1943

On New Year's Eve, 1942, General Eisenhower and General Montgomery, with his aid, Noel Chavasse, had dinner with Churchill and spent the night. Jock Colville recorded in his diary that "We saw the New Year in early so that General M. could go to bed. Punch was brewed, the P.M. made a little speech, the clerks, typists and some of the servants appeared and we formed a circle to sing 'Auld Lang Syne.' I was linked arm in arm with General Montgomery and the American barman."

## January, 1943

In January, 1943 allied leaders Churchill, Roosevelt and French Generals Charles de Gaulle and Henri Giraud met in Casablanca to discuss future plans for World War II, including the invasion of mainland Europe, the impending invasion of Sicily and Italy, and the wisdom of the principle of "unconditional surrender." Stalin was not present, saying he needed to stay in Russia because the Battle of Stalingrad required his attention and presence. During the conference, which lasted from January 14 to 24, Churchill strolled on the beach near the compound and came across a group of American sailors. "One of them had a guitar, and they were playing and singing," said an army photographer who recorded the story in the private Secret Service log of the conference. "The Prime Minister got in his car and started to drive off, but after a moment told his driver to stop and back up. When he got back to where the sailors were, Mr. Churchill stuck his head out of the window and said, 'How about playing me a tune?' Of course the sailors agreed, and they gathered around Mr. Churchill's car and sang him two songs, one of them being, 'You are My Sunshine.'" Author Jon Meacham noted that Churchill was "a fan of popular songs, the worse the better" and "loved it" when the sailors sang for him.

## Quebec Conference

When the Quebec Conference ended on August 24, 1943, Churchill took a holiday at La Cabane de Montmorency, a fishing camp in the Luarentian Mountains, which was put at his disposal by Canadian industrialist Colonel Frank Clarke. The following day he fished with his daughter, Mary, and worked on a broadcast he was scheduled to make to the Canadian people. Various members of the British delegation, who were at other lakeside cabins, motored over for lunch and dinner and on August 29 one of them noted, in his diary "Winston in terrific form, singing Dan Leno songs and other favourites of the Halls of forty years ago, together with the latest Noel Coward."

## Hit songs in England: 1943

The number one hit song in England during 1943 was "The White Cliffs of Dover." Also popular were "I'm Going to Get Lit Up When the Lights Go on in London" and "Shine On, Harvest Moon."

## Christmas and New Year's: 1943-1944

On December 3, 1943, American broadcaster Edward R. Murrow delivered his "Orchestrated Hell" broadcast over CBS Radio describing the Royal Air Force's nighttime bombing raid on Berlin. The next day Bolivia declared war on all Axis powers. The American VIII and XV Corps arrived in Europe and on Christmas Eve General Dwight D. Eisenhower was named the Supreme Allied Commander in Europe; two days later he was officially named head of Operation Overlord, the invasion of Normandy. A British cruiser sank the German battleship "Scharnhorst" in the Arctic.

At Chequers on Christmas Day, 1943, Churchill's daughter, Mary Soames, gave him "a complete set of Gilbert and Sullivan operas, which I knew he enjoyed—he would often, when in a jovial mood, sing ditties from his favourites." Two days after Christmas, Churchill went to Marrakesh, Morocco, for convalescence where he stayed at the Villa Taylor, the residence of the U.A. vice-consul.

On the evening of New Year's Day, Churchill "listened delightedly to two gramophone records of Gilbert and Sullivan operettas—*The Pirates of Penzance* and *Patience*—part of the set given to him for Christmas."

The next day, Churchill wrote to Mary, saying, "Darling Mary, Last night we played through 2 of yr records 'Pirates of Penzance' & 'Patience.' I read, and brooded on the flowing music. On the whole one of the happiest hours I have had in these hard days. How sweet of you to have had the impulse! How clever to have turned it into action & Fact. Your ever loving Father. W."

In his book, *Churchill Style: The Art of Being Winston Churchill*, author Barry Singer stated that "Churchill was notoriously nonmusical but loved to sing, particularly in the tub, and was always ready to dance unabashedly. One evening at Chequers after the films, he lassoed Field Marshall Alan Brooke into the Great Hall for sandwiches at 2:15 a.m. With the gramophone playing, Churchill, in one of his multi-colored silk dressing gowns, trotted round and round with a sandwich in one hand and watercress in the other, giving little skips to the tunes."

## EARLY 1944

On February 26, 1944, the "Big Week" bombing campaign over Germany began with American P-51 Mustang fighters protected by long range American bombers. On March 1 there were anti-fascist strikes in northern Italy and the Allies bombed the Vatican for the second time. In Anzio, Italy, Germany forces, unable to drive the Allies from their beachhead, went into a defensive position.

On Saturday, March 4, John Colville noted in his diary that "The P.M. in benevolent but somber mood. He is disturbed by the attitude of Russia—Stalin refused to be moderate about the Poles—and many other matters, political and strategic. He said that he felt like telling the Russians, 'Personally I fight tyranny whatever uniform it wears or slogans it utters.' Late at night, after the inevitable film, the P.M. took his station in the Great Hall and began to smoke Turkish cigarettes—the first time I have ever seen him smoke one—saying that they were the only thing he got out of the Turks. He keeps on reverting to the point that he has not long to live and tonight, while the gramophone played the 'Marseillaise' and 'Sambre et Meuse,'" he told his visitors that "this was his political testament for after the war: 'Far more important than India or the Colonies or solvency is the Air. We live in a world of wolves—and bears. Then we had to listen to most of Gilbert and Sullivan on the gramophone before retiring at 3.00 a.m."

## Clementine's Birthday

Mrs. Churchill's birthday was Saturday, April 1, 1944 and there was a family party with Duncan and Diana, Sarah, Mary and Jack. Jock Colville wanted to join the Royal Air Force and solicited Mary Soames and Mrs. Churchill for support. Colville stated in his diary that "The clocks were advanced to double summer time and we sat up till 4.30 while the P.M. worked. Duncan read important papers not intended for him to see and I played Gilbert and Sullivan and old music hall songs (which are the P.M.'s choice of music) on the gramophone."

On April 3, Allied bombers hit Budapest, Hungary, which was occupied by the Germans.

## Second Quebec Conference

On September 12, 1944, the Second Quebec Conference began; Roosevelt and Churchill discussed military cooperation in the Pacific and the future of Germany. On October 9 the Moscow Conference began with Churchill and Stalin discussing spheres of influence in the postwar Balkans and made the percentages agreement.

In November, 1944, British forces occupied Salonika, Greece and distributed food in Athens, which was experiencing famine while Axis forces left the Greek mainland for several Greek islands. President Franklin Roosevelt was elected to his fourth term on November 6. Zionist terrorists assassinated the British government representative in the Middle East. On November 9, General Patton's troops and tanks crossed the Moselle River and threatened Metz. German V-2 rockets continued to hit Britain and on November 20, Hitler left his wartime headquarters at Rastenberg, East Prussia and went to Berlin. Metz was taken on November 23 and in the Pacific, the United States forces were advancing. Heavy rains left the Italian front at a stalemate.

On December 1, it was "another exhausting morning, the P.M. having many engagements and much untouched work awaiting him," wrote Jock Colville in his diary. Still, "he went to Harrow for a school concert, accompanied by Mrs. Churchill" and others. "The songs were good," wrote Colville, "except for the 'school twelve' which was lamentable. A small boy, with a magnificent treble, sang 'Five Hundred Faces.' Afterwards there was a sherry party in the Headmaster's House, where the P.M. talked long and charmingly to the school monitors, such as he did to the midshipmen...last January, enthralling but never patronizing."

## YALTA CONFERENCE

The Yalta Conference began on February 4, 1945 and allied leaders Roosevelt, Stalin and Churchill gathered to discuss the reorganization of Europe after World War II. One of the controversial decisions at the conference was to allow Germany to be divided into communist and non-communist sections, which contributed to tensions during the Cold War.

On February 10, Churchill gave a dinner party for Roosevelt and Stalin at the Vorontsov Villa. After dinner, Churchill took Roosevelt and Stalin into his Map Room where the maps showed Soviet forces on the east bank of the Oder within thirty-eight miles of Berlin, British and Canadian forces on the western bank of the Rhine river, with American forces in the Philippines where they had entered Manila.

As they discussed the military situations, Stalin suggested that the British should consider making an armistice earlier than the Russians. Churchill, hurt and upset, moved to a corner of the Map Room where, with his hands in his pockets, he began to sing the opening lines of one of his favourite songs, "Keep right on to the end of the road." Stalin stood puzzled, then Roosevelt spoke up and, with a wide grin, said to the Russian interpreter "Tell your Chief that this singing by the Prime Minister is Britain's secret weapon."

# Keep Right On to the End of the Road

This song was written by Harry Lauder shortly after his son was killed in action during World War I.

Ev'ry road thro' life is a long, long road,
Fill'd with joys and sorrows too,
As you journey on how your heart will yearn
For the things most dear to you.
With wealth and love 'tis so,
But onward we must go.

CHORUS:
Keep right on to the end of the road,
Keep right on to the end,
Tho' the way be long, let your heart be strong,
Keep right on round the bend,
Tho' you're tird and weary still journey on,
Till you come to your happy abode,
Where all the love you've been dreaming of
Will be there at the end of the road.

With a big stout heart to a long steep hill,
We may get there with a smile,
With a good kind thought and an end in view,
We may cut short many a mile.
So let courage ev'ry day
Be your guiding star always

CHORUS:

## HARRY LAUDER

Harry Lauder was born in Edinburgh, Scotland in 1870 and became a popular music hall singer and comedian. His biggest hit was "I Love a Lassie" and Churchill once called him "Scotland's greatest ever ambassador." Other well known songs of his include "Roamin' in the Gloamin" and "A Wee Deoch-an-Doris."

During his 20s, Lauder worked in the coal mines and often sang for the miners, then began performing in Music Halls where his repertoire included comedic songs and songs of Scotland and Ireland.

He turned professional by 1894 and became famous performing at the Charring Cross Music Hall and the London Pavilion. He wrote "I Love a Lassie" when he was performing at the Theatre Royal in Glasgow in a Howard & Wyndham pantomime; the song made him a national star.

At one time, Lauder was the highest paid performer in the world. During World War I, he toured the U.K. and promoted recruitment into the services and also performed numerous concerts for troops at home and on the western front.

Lauder's son, John, a graduate of Cambridge University was killed in action on December 28, 1916. That led Lauder to write "The End of the Road." Churchill said that Lauder, "by his inspiring songs and valiant life, rendered measureless service to the Scottish race and to the British Empire."

Lauder retired in 1935 but during World War II entertained troops throughout Britain and made wireless broadcasts on the BBC with the Scottish Symphony Orchestra. A native Scotsman, Lauder was known for performing in kilts with a walking stick.

Lauder wrote most of the songs he performed and "The End of the Road" is still used by the Birmingham City Football Club as their club anthem.

Harry Lauder died on February 26, 1950 at the age of 80. At his funeral, the Queen Mother and Winston Churchill both sent large wreaths.

## February, 1945

On February 13 and 14, 1945, Dresden was firebombed by Allied air forces and large parts of the historic city were damaged.

The next day, Jock Colville recorded in his diary that "After dinner we saw an amusing film: Bob Hope in *The Princess and the Pirate*, a comedy which featured co-star Virginia Mayo singing 'Kiss Me in the Moonlight.'"

"Then we sat in the Great Hall and listened to the Mikado played, much too slowly, on the gramophone," continued Colville. "The P.M. said it brought back 'the Victorian era, eighty years which will rank in our island history with the Antonine age.' Now, however, 'the shadows of victory' were upon us. In 1940 the issue was clear and he could see distinctly what was to be done. But when Bert Harris finished talking about the destruction of Germany, Churchill asked 'What will lie between the white snows of Russia and the white cliffs of Dover?' Perhaps, however the Russians would not want to sweep on to the Atlantic or something might stop them as the accident of Genghis Khan's death had stopped the horsed archers of the Mongols, who retired and never came back.

Bert Harris: 'You mean now they will come back?; W.S.C.: 'Who can say? They may not want to. But there is an unspoken fear in many people's hearts.' After this war, continued the P.M., we should be weak, we should have no money and no strength and we should lie between the two great powers of the U.S.A. and the U.S.S.R. If he lived, he should concentrate on one thing: the air. Harris replied that it would have to be rockets: 'The bomber is a passing phase and, like the battleship, it has nearly passed.' 'Then, said the P.M., you mean we must make our island into a volcano.'"

Churchill then quoted "Ye Mariners of England" at length, a ballad written by Thomas Campbell that begins

Ye Mariners of England
That guard our native seas;
Whose flag has braved, a thousand years,
The battle and the breeze!
Your glorious standard launch again
To match another foe,
And sweep through the deep,
While the stormy winds do blow;
While the battle rages loud and long,
And the stormy winds do blow

Bert Harris said, "That was written before the invention of the 12,000 lb bomb." Churchill countered, "Ye Doodle Bugs of England that guard our native seas..."

Here are the verses to some other Music Hall songs that Churchill sang:

I wanted to get married
Like a lot of foolish men
Found a girl, got engaged
Got married there and then
But after it was over
I'd got taken down a peg
Her hair, her eyes, her teeth
Were false
And she'd a wooden leg
But I can't change it
I can't change it
It was a great surprise to me
Half a woman and half a tree
But I'll chop her up for firewood
In the sweet by and by.

And then there was:

I've been to the North Pole
I've been to the South Pole
The East Pole, the West Pole
And every other kind of pole
The Barber's Pole
The greasy Pole
And I'm fairly up the Pole
Since I got the sack
From the Hotel Metropole

## CHURCHILL LOSES ELECTION

On February 24, 1945, there was massive bombing of Germany by approximately 9,000 bombers. That same day Egypt declared war on the Axis. On April 16, the Soviets overtook Berlin and Hitler committed suicide on April 30. Germany surrendered to the Allies on May 7 and the next day, May 8, was declared "V-E Day."

On July 26, Winston Churchill was defeated by Clement Atlee in the general election with a majority of voters naming social reform, such as the housing crisis, as their primary concern and their belief that Atlee was a better choice to lead those efforts.

The Potsdam Conference began on July 17 with Churchill in attendance with Stalin and President Harry Truman, who had replaced Roosevelt after the latter died on April 12. Churchill was soon replaced by Atlee at the conference.

On July 28, Churchill's daughter Mary was with him at Chequers and "saw with near desperation a cloud of black doom descend." She and Sarah played him his favourite Gilbert and Sullivan records but his mood would not lighten. Then, they played some French and American marches, which helped a bit, and then "Run Rabbit Run" and "The Wizard of Oz" which cheered him up.

## The Wizard of Oz

"The Wonderful Wizard of Oz" was a novel by L. Frank Baum, released in 1900. The book was popular and there were several film versions before the classic, starring Judy Garland, was released at the end of 1939. The film score was written by Harold Arlen (music) and Edgar "Yip" Harburg (lyrics). The film won Academy Awards for "Best Film Score" and "Best Original Song" for "Over the Rainbow."

Other songs in the classic musical are "If I Only Had a Heart," "Ding-Dong! The Witch is Dead," "Follow the Yellow Brick Road" and "We're Off to See the Wizard."

## The End of World War II

The United States dropped an atomic bomb on the Japanese cities of Hiroshima on August 6 and Nagasaki on August 8, the same day the Soviet Union declared war on Japan and invaded Manchuria. Japan's formal surrender came on September 2 when the document was signed on the deck of the USS Missouri in Tokyo Bay. On September 4, the last German troops surrendered and the next day Singapore was liberated by British and Indian troops.

## PAINTING

On September 6, Field Marshall Alexander joined Churchill at his villa at Lake Como in Lombardo, Italy. Churchill had flown down on the Prime Minister's plane, which Attlee had placed at his disposal, on September 2. Churchill was accompanied by his daughter, Sarah, while Clementine remained at Chartwell, which had been neglected during the war years. Churchill had acquired a new London home at 28 Hyde Park Gate and Clementine wanted to prepare it for them to reside.

Churchill and Alexander painted together, using a speedboat to cross the lake for quiet bays. Four days before the Churchill's thirty-seventh wedding anniversary, he painted and then took control of the speedboat as it traveled back to his villa. That evening, he wrote to Clementine, "When I was driving the speed-boat back, there came into my mind your singing to me 'In the Gloaming' years ago. What a sweet song & tune & how beautifully you sang it in all its pathos. My heart fills with love to feel you near me in thought. I feel so tenderly towards you my darling & the more pleasant & agreeable the scenes & days, the more I wish you were here to share them & give me a kiss."

# Roamin' in the Gloamin'(1911)

I've seen lots o'bonnie lassies trav'llin' far and wide,
But my heart is centered on bonnie Kate McBride.
And altho' I'm no' a chap that throws a word away,
I'm surprised mysel' sometimes at a 'I've got to say.

CHORUS
Roamin' in the gloamin' On the bonnie banks o'Clyde,
Roamin' in the gloamin' wae my lassie by my side.
When the sun as gone to rest
That's the time that we love best.
O, it's lovely roamin' in the gloamin'!

One nicht in the gloamin' we were trippin' side by side;
I kissed her twice, and asked her once if she would be my bride
She was shy, so was I, we were baith the same,
But I got brave and braver on the journey comin' hame.

Last nicht efter strollin' we got hame at half-past nine;
Sittin' at the kitchen fire I asked her to be mine.
When she promised, I got up and danced the Hielan 'fling.
I've just been at the jew'ler's and I've picked a nice wee ring

## Back at Harrow

In October, 1945, Churchill was back at Harrow where he gave a speech to the students and told them that he had been "much attracted" to the kettledrum and often thought, "If only I could get hold of this on one of these fine evenings." That opportunity never came "So I gave up that ambition and transferred my aspirations to another part of the orchestra. I thought, 'If I cannot have the kettle-drum I might try to be the conductor.' There was a great deal in the gestures, at any rate." That did not happen while he was at Harrow "but eventually, after a great deal of perseverance, I rose to be conductor of quite a considerable band. It was a very large band and it played with very strange and formidable instruments, and the roar and thunder of its music resounded throughout the world."

## Films

The downstairs dining room at Chartwell was converted into a movie theater; Churchill was "addicted" to films, especially musicals. Every other night, his staff chose a film and Churchill always wanted an audience with him to watch. In his book, *In Search of Churchill*, author Martin Gilbert wrote, "Miss Hamblin told me. 'All the outdoor staff and the indoor staff would be invited. We would all be seated. He would come in after dinner, like the Queen, and he would say, 'Let her go.' After each film the lights would go up and the others would wait for Churchill to comment. Once, after watching *Wuthering*

*Heights*, he was silent for quite a while, then piped up: 'What terrible weather they have in Yorkshire.' A favourite film was *Lady Hamilton*, with Vivien Leigh and Laurence Olivier. When it was first released in the United States in 1941, with the title *That Hamilton Woman*, Churchill advised Alexander Korda by telegram to change the title for the United Kingdom release, and Korda did so. The film brought Churchill to tears: Nelson's patriotism in exile was portrayed in the very language of Churchill's wilderness years, the very years when Chartwell had hummed the most."

Chips Gemmell, who had joined Churchill's secretarial team, stated about the evening films at Chartwell, "He loved the films, any film. After it, tears down his face, then wiping them way, "The best film I've ever seen."

## Iron Curtain Speech

During September, 1945, Churchill spent 25 days painting in Italy—and completed 15 paintings—then returned to his home at 28 Hyde Park Gate. Waiting for him were numerous invitations he had received, including one from President Harry Truman to do three or four lectures at Westminster College in Fulton, Missouri. Churchill agreed to deliver one lecture.

The Churchills had decided to spend the winter of 1946 in Miami and on January 13 arrived in New York, then traveled to Miami. On February 10, Churchill had dinner with President Truman and Secretary of State James Byrnes at the White House and discussed the theme of his speech.

Churchill missed the active involvement in world affairs that he was part of as Prime Minister but read newspapers to keep up with current events.

Two days later, Churchill hosted a lunch for General Eisenhower at the British Embassy in Washington, then retuned to Miami.

On March 1, Churchill took a train from Miami to Washington and three days later, accompanied by President Truman and Admiral Leahy, who was Roosevelt's personal Chief of Staff during World War II and then continued in that role for Truman, traveled by train to Missouri.

During the 24 hour overnight train trip, Churchill worked on his speech.

On March 5, in the gymnasium of the private, all male Westminster College, Churchill delivered his famous "iron curtain" speech. In that speech he confronted the issue of Europe's division between Communist and democratic spheres, nothing that an "iron curtain" separated the "free" countries from those under Communism.

The speech was broadcast live and had an immediate impact. The phrase "iron curtain" entered the political lexicon and was a defining description of the Cold War.

# Seventy-fourth Birthday

For Winston Churchill's seventy-fourth birthday on November 30, 1948, his family invited singer and actress Audrey Cleaver to sing some of his favorite songs to him. The family asked Churchill to list his favorite songs and the list included:

We're so glad to see you back again, dear lady
Naughty, naughty the Gerard
Keep the Home Fires Burning
The Long, Long, Trail
In the gloaming, oh my darling
If you were the only girl in the world, and I were the only boy
On the Mississippi
When the midnight choo choo leaves for Alabam
Oh Listen to the Band
Life on the Ocean Wave
Destiny waltz
Soldiers of the Queen
Tipperary
The Harrow School Song—Forty Years On
Land of Hope and Glory
Lilly of Laguna

And "anything by Ginger Rogers & Fred Astaire and Noel Coward tunes."

## Prime Minister Again

In October, 1951, Winston Churchill was elected Prime Minister again, defeating Clement Atlee. In his diary, John Colville wrote, "Circumstances in 1951 were totally different from those existing in 1945, but Churchill began by trying to re-create the situation as he had left it six years before..... When Winston Churchill wanted something and chose to exercise his persuasive gift, there were few who found it possible to refuse. Thus 'Auld Lang Syne' was ringing out along the Whitehall corridors and I suppose that I myself was a small part of the refrain."

On Tuesday, May 6, 1952, Churchill was at Strasbourg, France and "wanted to see British, American, German and French contingents march past him," wrote John Colville, "each to their own national songs: in creating international unity, national marching songs could play a great part."

Colville noted that "In lighter moments he could, and did, still quote verses of poetry, sing the music-hall songs of the 1890s and discourse learnedly on the American Civil War or the campaigns of Marlborough and Prince Eugene."

In 1955, Churchill, who was 80, resigned as Prime Minister and was succeeded by Anthony Eden.

## HARROW: 1964

In 1964, Churchill returned to Harrow where the boys "sang '"Forty years on."' Cecile Sandys wrote, "The eighteen-year-old Winston could hardly have imagined, as he left Harrow after an undistinguished time there, that seventy-two years later on his ninetieth birthday a new generation of boys would be singing a specially written verse to honour their most famous pupil.

"Blazoned with honour! For each generation
You kindled courage to stand and to stay;
You led our fathers to fight for the nation,
Called "Follow up" and yourself showed the way.
We who were born in the calm after thunder
Cherish our freedom to think and to do;
If in our turn we forgetfully wonder,
Yet we'll remember we owe it to you."

## LEAVES POLITICAL LIFE

In 1964, Churchill did not run for re-election to Parliament and effectively retired from politics.

## DEATH

Winston Churchill died on January 24, 1965 at his home at 28 Hyde Park Gate. He was 90 and had suffered a stroke.

It was the seventieth anniversary of his father's death.

# FUNERAL

Winston Churchill's funeral was the largest state funeral in world history, attended by representatives from 112 countries.

The funeral procession had a gun carriage to carry Churchill's coffin from Westminster Hall to St. Paul's accompanied by marching bands of the British Armed Forces, who played, slowly with muffled drums, Handel's "Dear March from Saul," Chopin's "Funeral March," three selections from Beethoven, "Funeral March No. 1," "Funeral March No. 2" and "Funeral March No. 3," Mendelssohn's "Funeral Marge," "Funeral March Regrets" by Panne, "Song of Death" by Sommer and "Vanished Army" by Alford.

During the service in St. Paul's, the hymns "Who Would True Valor See" (commonly known as "To Be a Pilgrim"), "The Battle Hymn of the Republic," "Fight the Good Fight With All Your Might," then "Last Post" and "Reveille" were sung.

Shortly after his death, daughter Sarah wrote to her brother, Randolph, and "recalled the poetry their father liked: 'Heroic poetry, poems with stories and legends. But there were other facets to his enjoyment, such as his appreciation of beauty—a compassion for humanity, as is embraced by the wryly humorous and philosophical ditties of Chesterton, Lear and music-hall songs.'"

## GRAMOPHONE RECORDS DISCOVERED

A number of years back—it was probably around 2007 or so—I asked the Churchill Archive in Cambridge via email what gramophone records owned by Winston Churchill were in their archive. I was curious because I knew Churchill loved music and thought he probably owned gramophone records of popular songs but was surprised to learn that the collection in the archive consisted primarily of recordings of his speeches.

Then I learned in 2013 that a wooden box had been discovered in Churchill's study that contained a number of gramophone records. Apparently, no one had previously thought to look in that cabinet.

In that box there were recordings of Churchill's speeches but there were also "popular" recordings such as "A.P. Herbert: to entertain you with some of his witty amusing and satirical verses" which included "Vital statistics," "Burglars Beware!" and "The King's regulation." There was a "humorous monologue by Arthur Marshall" that included "a nature walk," "the hostel," "showing the school" and "the games mistress." There was "Chuck it, Priestly" by Dr. Charles Hill" and "humorous monologues by Stanley Holloway."

There was a medley of Leslie Stuart's songs, "The Lost Chord" and "In the gloaming," an "album of popular songs," "A Time to Sing," "The White Cliffs of Dover" by Lynn Fontanne, Aleta Roberts Slater singing "I will come back in the spring" and "Rally round for freedom." "The Churchill Song" by Edgar Fawcett (lyrics) and H. Baynton-Power sung by Raymond

Newell. There was "The Cuckoo Waltz" and "Nights of Gladness Waltz," "Paul Robeson Medley No. 2," "Chu Chin Chow selection," "The Road to the Isles" and "Keep Right On to the End of the Road" by Sir Harry Lauder, 18 songs from "The King and I," "Vocal gems" from "The Arcadians" and "Veronique."

There was Noel Coward singing "Don't let's be beastly to the Germans" and "The Welcoming land." There were "humorous monologues by Stanley Holloway and songs performed by Kenneth McKellar. There were records of "Me and My Melinda" and "Johnny Doughboy found a rose in Ireland," "Aboard the Windjammer," the Australian songs "Waltzing Matilda" and "Waiata Poi," Noel Coward singing "I'm old Fashioned" and "You'd Be so nice to come home to," "Let's all join in the chorus with Tommy Handley and his pals" and "comic songs with Margaret Rutherford and Frankie Howard."

That list of gramophone records showed that Winston Churchill loved to be entertained by music. He loved the Gilbert and Sullivan operas but also loved the Music Hall songs. If he were a contemporary American, his taste in music would probably lean to country music, a genre that, like the Music Hall songs of nineteenth century England, are written and performed for ordinary, everyday, working class citizens. Like Music Hall songs, country music songs are often disparaged by the upper class while many in that class secretly enjoy them as a guilty pleasure.

Winston Churchill felt absolutely no guilt in loving—and singing—Music Hall songs.

# SOURCES

"Winston has learned a new song..." (The Young Churchill by Celia Sandy, p. 31)

"learned words and manners which were highly unsuitable for a young gentleman"... (Sandys, p. 58)

"reacted with shock and apprehension..." (Sandys, p. 58)

"At Brighton, young Churchill discovered concerts... Celia Sandys. P ??? (Singer?)

"there is a ripping good Pantomine down here..." Sandys

"Winston favored music hall tunes... (Singer, 23)

"as a woman 'Lady Bertha' & he acted..." (Sandys, 69).

"a pantomime in Brighton where they hissed..." (Sandys, 91)

"I am going to a play called 'Pinafore'... (Sandys) (104)

"To have an exciting story told..." (Sandys 121)

"It was very amusing he astonished ... (Sandys, 121)

"Colonel Gouraud, received a "Perfected Phonograph..." (*The Guinness Book of Recorded Sound* by Robert and Celia Dearling with Brian Rust.. p. 26)

"the world's first "live" recording..." (Dearling, p. 215)

"I rank as one of the most prominent trebles... (Sandys, 118)

"Winston was not to look back... Sandys

"always enjoyed the Harrow songs..." (Sandys, 111)

"of which Mrs. Ormiston Chant is a fair specimen... (Sandys, p. 210) "organization founded with the express purpose"... (Sandys, p. 210)

"surprised and a little disconcerted at the dingy...(Sandys, p. 210)

"encountered a side of life that he...." (Sandys, p. 210)

"Mrs. Ormiston Chant and her 'prowling prudes'... (Sandys, 210)

"I can assure you I have very... (*Churchill Speaks* by Robert Rhodes James, p. 153)

"bought a Welte Steinway piano..."(*Churchill Style: The Art of Being Winston Churchill* by Barry Singer, p. 119)

"he again bought on installment..." (Singer, p. 119)

"Winston Churchill was the world's most.." (94)

"All his life, Churchill enjoyed singing..." (*In Search of Churchill: A historian journey* by Martin Gilbert. P. 95-95)

"In his old age Churchill wanted to..." (Gilbert: *In Search of*, p. 95)

"I drink champagne at all meals..." (Singer, 111)

"each night he would turn out the lights..." (*Churchill: A Life* by Martin Gilbert, p. 482)

"it was a need to dance..." (London at War by Philip Ziegler)

"Customers want to dance..." (Ziegler, p (51)

"There were more dance bands playing..." (Ziegler, p. 51)

"It was at once the most dramatic...." (*The Fringes of Power: The Incredible Inside Story of Winston Churchill During World War II* by John Colville, p. ???

"It was light and deliciously warm..." Colville

“He was in high spirits, repeating poetry....” (Colville, p. 157-158)

“he sang ‘Ole Man River’ (out of tune)...” (Colville, p. 227)

“The stirring patriotism these verses... “ ????

“Listening to those boys singing all those...” (Gilbert, *Churchill*, p. 20)

“at the top of his voice.” (Kendall)

“what an inspiration the Harrow songs...” (Kendall, p. 96/29)

”the shorthand writer was dismissed...” (Gilbert, *Churchill*, p. 686)

“another sort of sing-song until after midnight.” (Gilbert: In Search of, p. 183-184)

“We must be the arsenal of democracy.”... (Gilbert, Churchill, p. 688)

“all American tunes or ones with...” (Gilbert, Churchill, p. 689)

“the gramophone played and the P.M....” (Colville, 344)

“flippant conversation about metaphysics... (Colville, 364)

“moving spirit behind Japan’s decision” (Colville, 369-370)

“Will Germany, without the command... (Colville, 369-370)

“was now sure Germany would attack.... (Colville, 369-370)

“arrived for dinner, at which... (Colville, 374)

“to desist from the unilateral imposition... (Gilbert, *Churchill*, p. 837-838)

“not supported in the House or... (Colville, p. 412)

“till 2 a.m. while I played the gramophone...” (Colville, p. 412)

“thought that when the war was over... (Colville, p. 412)

"The P.M. inveighed against defeatism... (Colville, p. 412

"after the Franco-Germany Armistice... (Colville, p. 412)

"The reactions to the Churchill-Roosevelt... (Colville, p. 427)

"about Harrow, where he said he had spent... (Colville, p. 444)

"Almost a year has passed since..." (James, pp. 771-772)

"We must learn to be equally good..." (James, pp. 771-772)

"Another lesson I think we may take..." (James, pp. 771-772)

"You sang here a verse..." (James, pp. 771-772)

"There is one word in it I want to alter..." (James, pp. 771-772)

"Do not let us speak of darker days..." (James, pp. 771-772)

"We did not make this war, we did not..." (James, p. 786)

"that great man whom destiny has marked..." (James, p. 787)

"There shall be no halting, or half measures..." (James, p. 788)

"That grand old minstrel, Harry Lauder...." (James, p. 788)

"When I warned them that Britain would..." (James, p. 788)

"We saw the New Year in early so that..." (Colville, p. 459)

"One of them had a guitar, and they were playing..." (Meacham, p. 207)

"The Prime Minister got in his car..." (Meacham, p. 208)

"Winston in terrific form, singing..." (Gilbert, *Churchill*, p. 752)

"a complete set of Gilbert and Sullivan operas..." (*A Daughter's Tale: The Memoir of Winston Churchill's Youngest Child* by Mary Soames, p. 266)

"listened delightedly to two gramophone records..." (Singer, 181)

"Darling Mary, Last night we played..." (Soames, p. 266)

"Churchill was notoriously nonmusical..." (Singer, 176)

"The P.M. in benevolent but somber mood..." (Colville, p. 476-477)

"The clocks were advanced to double summer..." (Colville, p. 482)

"another exhausting morning, the P.M...." (Colville, p. 531)

"Tell your Chief that this singing..." (Gilbert, *Churchill*, p. 822)

"by his inspiring songs and valiant life.." (James, p. 787)

"After dinner we saw an amusing..." (Colville, p. 563-564)

"Then we sat in the Great Hall and listened..." (Colville, p. 563-564)

"That was written before the invention..." (Colville, p. 563-564)

"saw with near desperation a cloud of..." (Gilbert, *Churchill*, p. 856)

"When I was driving the speed-boat back..." (Gilbert, *Churchill*, p. 859)

"If only I could get hold of this..." (Gilbert, *Churchill*, p. 20)

"Miss Hamblin told me. 'All the outdoor..." (Gilbert: In Search of, p. 312.

"He loved the films, any film..." (Gilbert: In Search of, p. 312)

"Circumstances in 1951 were totally..." (Colville, p. 633)

"wanted to see British, American..." (Colville, p. 646)

“In lighter moments he could, and...” (Colville, p. 635)

“sang “‘Forty years on.’...” (Sandys, p. 175)

“recalled the poetry their father liked...” (Gilbert: In Search of, p. 208)

# Selected Bibliography


Baldwin, Neil. *Edison: Inventing the Century*. New York: Hyperion, 1995.

Bergreen, Laurence. *As Thousands Cheer: The Life of Irving Berlin*. New York: Viking, 1990.

Churchill, Winston S. *Memoirs of the Second World War*. Boston: Houghton Mifflin, 1959, 1987.

Colville, John. *The Fringes of Power: The Incredible Inside Story of Winston Churchill During World War II*. Guilford, CT: The Lyons Press, 1985.

Dearling, Robert & Celia with Brian Rust. *The Guinness Book of Recorded Sound*. Middlesex, England: Guinness, 1984.

Gilbert and Sullivan, Wikipedia

Gilbert, Martin. *Churchill: A Life*. New York: Henry Holt and Company, 1991.

Gilbert, Martin. *In Search of Churchill: A historian's journey*. New York: John Wiley & Sons, Inc., 1994.

James, Robert Rhodes. *Churchill Speaks: 1897-1963: Collected Speeches in Peace & War*. Chelsea House Publishers, 1980.

Kendall, Jill. "Churchill and Music," *The Finest Hour*, number 96.

Langworth, Richard M. *Winston Churchill, Myth and reality: What He Actually Did and Said*. Jefferson, N.C.: McFarland and Company, 2017.

Lauder, Harry. Wikipedia.

Lincoln & Churchill Musical Tastes. Lincolnandchurchill.org/musical-taste

Lukacs, John. *Five Days in London: May 1940*. New Haven: Yale University Press, 1999.

Meacham, Jon. *Franklin and Winston: An Intimate Portrait of an Epic Friendship*. New York: Random House, 2004.

Michaels, Sean. "Winston Churchill's speeches weren't always so popular." *Daily Telegraph*.

Olson, Lynne. *Citizens of London: The Americans Who Stood With Britain in Its Darkest, Finest, Hour*. New York: Random House, 2010

Sandys, Celia. *The Young Churchill: The Early Years of Winston Churchill*. Dutton: A William Abrahams Book: New York and London, 1994.

Shilling, Jane. "Churchill's Secret Cabinet and Some in the Arms of God. *The Daily Telegraph*, July 10, 2013.

Singer, Barry. *Churchill Style: The Art of Being Winston Churchill*. New York: Abrams Image, 2012.

Soames, Mary, editor. *Speaking for Themselves: The Personal Letters of Winston and Clementine Churchill*. London: Doubleday, 1998.

Soames, Mary. *A Daughter's Tale: The Memoir of Winston Churchill's Youngest Child*. New York: Random House, 2011.

Ziegler, Philip. *London At War: 1939-1945*. New York: Alfred A. Knopf, 1995.

CPSIA information can be obtained
at www.ICGtesting.com
Printed in the USA
LVOW13*2152080318
569220LV00001B/4/P

9 780999 053713